I Get It!

Discovering How to Really Live in the Promises of God

J. Clay Stevens

Copyright © 2014 by J. Clay Stevens

I GET IT!
Discovering How To Really Live In The Promises Of God
by J. Clay Stevens

Printed in the United States of America

Edited by Xulon Press

ISBN 9781498413824

All rights reserved solely by the author. The author guarantees all contents are original and do not infringe upon the legal rights of any other person or work. No part of this book may be reproduced in any form without the permission of the author. The views expressed in this book are not necessarily those of the publisher.

Scripture quotations taken from the New American Standard Bible (NASB). Copyright © 1960, 1962, 1963, 1968, 1971, 1972, 1973, 1975, 1977, 1995 by The Lockman Foundation. Used by permission. All rights reserved.

Scripture quotations taken from the New International Version (NIV). Copyright © 1973, 1978, 1984, 2011 by Biblica, Inc.™. Used by permission. All rights reserved.

Scripture quotations taken from the New Century Version (NCV). Copyright © 2005 by Thomas Nelson, Inc. Used by permission. All rights reserved.

Scripture quotations taken from the New Living Translation (NLT). Copyright © 1996, 2004, 2007 by Tyndale House Foundation. Used by permission. All rights reserved.

Scripture quotations taken from the Contemporary English Version (CEV). Copyright © 1995 American Bible Society. Used by permission. All rights reserved.

www.xulonpress.com

To Deborah & Michael,
Your hard work and contributions to this project have been a great blessing. Your growth as followers of Jesus manifests itself to all those around you. Cindi & I love you guys. Go get all that God has for you!

Pastor Clay

To Cindi

Your unconditional love, unwavering faith, and unending support make life with you unbelievable and life without you unimaginable.

You have made this book and my ministry possible.

Thank you for loving Jesus more than you love me and for loving me more than I deserve.

TABLE OF CONTENTS

Acknowledgments ix
Introduction. xi

Chapter 1: What Is It?. 19
Chapter 2: Why Don't I Have It? 31
Chapter 3: Do I Really Want It? 43
Chapter 4: Where Does It Come From?. 49
Chapter 5: How Do I Begin to Get It? 59
Chapter 6: Am I in Position for It?. 75
Chapter 7: Am I Prepared for It? 87
Chapter 8: How Do I Plan for It? 103
Chapter 9: Will I Know When I Get It? 113

Endnotes 125

Acknowledgments

This book is a result of the investment and input of many people, too many to be able to name them all—men and women who invested in me in the early days of my walk with Jesus, pastors I have served under, professors who taught me, and authors whose writings have instructed and inspired me. These would be just a few.

But just because there's not enough time or space to list everyone who has helped to shape me and my ministry doesn't mean that I shouldn't acknowledge some who have had a significant impact on my life and on this project.

Dr. Charles Stanley, whom I talk about in the introduction. He not only helped shape my early days as a follower of Jesus, but because of his selfless act of having dinner with one young seminary student and his wife, he gave me the inspiration for *I Get It!*

Hinton Harris, one of my pastoral mentors, who gave me the pulpit every Sunday night and allowed me to cut my preaching teeth on his flock. I'm sure it was at times a painful experience for the men and women of Emmanuel Baptist Church, but I am eternally grateful for his gracious gift.

First Baptist Church in Waverly, Tennessee, and Pastor Paul Tirey, who gave me my first shot at vocational ministry.

First Baptist Church in Okeechobee, Florida, and Pastor Dick Whipple, who ordained me for the gospel ministry and gave me a love for God's Word.

Debra Martin, who edited my manuscript and offered helpful suggestions for the clarification of some of the ideas shared. Also, my brother, Hawley, and my friend Erik Clary, who read the manuscript and shared constructive thoughts and insights. And my mom, who prayed for me and was willing to do whatever was necessary to see this book birthed.

The amazing people of Cross Culture Church, who support me in more ways than can be imagined. You bless me by coming back week after week and allowing me the privilege of being God's messenger boy to you. Most of the stories and concepts shared in this book, you've probably heard me share from the platform. The spiritual truths fleshed out in sermons became the foundation for much of the content of this book. Words cannot express the gratitude I have for you.

Foremost, I acknowledge the God who loved me so much that He would rather die than live without me. So He did. He laid down His life so that I could take up the eternal life that Jesus paid for. It is the abundant life. He gave it so that we could get it.

INTRODUCTION

Certain events stick with us as long as we live. Some of the events are tragic, such as the terrorist attacks of September 11, 2001. Almost everyone who was alive then and old enough to know what was happening can tell you where they were and what they were doing when they heard the words, "A plane just flew into the World Trade Center!"

Some of the events of our lives are joyous, such as our wedding day or the birth of a child. There is such joy and excitement associated with these types of events that our minds easily recall them. We want those types of memories. We invite them into our crowded and often stressful lives because they provide a respite for our minds and a safe haven for our thoughts.

And some events that appear to come into our lives as a matter of coincidence end up shaping our lives in such a profound way that we can't help but believe that the providence of God has brought us to that moment. Memories of those events are also etched permanently in our minds. It was just such an event that inspired the writing of this book and shaped the course of my calling and ministry.

It was March 30, 1998, and I was attending Southeastern Baptist Theological Seminary in Wake Forest, North Carolina.

My wife, Cindi, was the administrative assistant to the dean of students. Cindi was responsible for arranging the lodging and transportation for all the guest chapel speakers. That meant that I got to pick up most of them from the airport, take them to dinner, and then deliver them to their rooms. It was an incredible honor for me to have the opportunity to spend time with some of the great spiritual leaders of our time.

Dr. Charles Stanley had accepted an invitation to speak in a chapel service at Southeastern. I was excited at the prospect of meeting him. Dr. Stanley, long-time pastor of First Baptist Church in Atlanta and founder of InTouch Ministries, had already been a huge influence in my life and walk with Jesus. Cindi and I, along with some friends, used to go back to our house after church on Sunday nights and watch Dr. Stanley on television. Then we would sit around talking about his message and its implications for our lives as followers of Jesus. He has a way of communicating God's Word that seems so clear and simple and, at the same time, thought-provoking and profound.

But alas, it seemed it was not meant to be. In this instance, the president of our seminary was out of town and would not be back until later that night, but he had instructed the dean of students to pick up Dr. Stanley personally. I'm sure Dr. Patterson, our seminary president, wanted to make sure that an overexcited seminary student didn't pounce on Dr. Stanley with a thousand questions. However, because of circumstances beyond his control—I like to think it was divine intervention—the dean of students, at the last minute, was unable to go to the airport, and I was dispatched to Raleigh-Durham International to meet Dr. Charles Stanley. Did I mention I was excited?

As we stood at baggage claim waiting for his checked bag and talking small talk, I noticed out of the corner of my eye a woman staring at us—well, more precisely, staring at Dr. Stanley. You could tell that she was trying to figure out if this was who she thought it was. Dr. Stanley and his InTouch Ministries have reached and continue to reach millions of people around the world every week.

Finally the woman got up enough nerve to come over to where we were standing. Sheepishly she inquired, "Dr. Stanley?"

"Yes ma'am," Dr. Stanley responded. Even before the words were completely out of his mouth, tears were streaming down this woman's face, and as she reached out her hand she said, "I've always wanted to meet the man who changed my life."

As I said, InTouch is a television, radio, and print ministry that reaches around the globe and has made Dr. Charles Stanley one of the most recognized pastor/preachers of our time. I have no doubt that many such encounters like that one at the baggage claim have occurred throughout Dr. Stanley's ministry. But with what I perceived was a genuine show of humility, Dr. Stanley seemed caught off guard by this woman's emotionally charged expression of gratitude. She began to share her story with Dr. Stanley as if she'd known him all her life.

The conversation between the two of them went on for no more than four or five minutes before she was on her way with her luggage—and no doubt a great story for her Sunday school class. I'm sure she felt a deep sense of appreciation for the chance to meet this man who obviously had impacted her spiritual journey in a unique and powerful way. I was feeling the same way.

My wife had already informed me that it had been arranged for Dr. Stanley to have dinner that night with a couple who were supporters of his ministry, so as I escorted Dr. Stanley to his room, I reminded him what time chapel was held and told him that everyone was looking forward to hearing him speak in the morning. It had already been a great honor for me to meet Dr. Stanley. Like the woman at the airport, this man's ministry had changed my life, but what happened next is as fresh in my mind as if it happened yesterday.

As I turned to leave the room, Dr. Stanley said, "Clay, what am I supposed to do about dinner?"

I responded, "Dr. Stanley, it's my understanding that your office has arranged for you to have dinner tonight with a couple who live in this area and who are supporters of your ministry."

To this, Dr. Stanley replied, "Yes, I think that's right, but I don't want to do that. I want to have dinner with you and your wife."

Close your mouth, Clay! Pick yourself up off the floor, Clay! Snap out of it, Clay! Say something, Clay! "Uh, well, Dr. Stanley, I really appreciate that, and it would be a great honor, but I'm sure that there are plenty of professors on campus who would love to take you to dinner."

This next part still amazes me every time I think about it. Dr. Charles Stanley, pastor of one of the largest churches in America, with a radio, television, and print ministry that has touched millions of lives, said to me, a second-year seminary student, "No, I want to go to dinner with you and your wife. I think I could learn something from you." *Close your mouth, Clay! Pick yourself up off the floor, Clay! Snap out . . .* Well, you get the picture.

I'll never forget calling Cindi and saying, "Get ready. We're going to dinner with Charles Stanley!"

As we sat there that evening over dinner, the conversation flowed surprisingly freely. Dr. Stanley talked openly and candidly about his life and ministry, and as he did, he would periodically intersperse questions to me about my ministry. What was my purpose in ministry? What did I want to accomplish? What kind of pastor did I want to be? What kind of communicator of God's Word? What kind of ministry did I want to have? How was I going to impact lives?

Introduction

Each question seemed to probe a little deeper and cause me to look a little harder at my purpose in ministry. I knew God had given me a deep passion to communicate His Word. I knew I needed to prepare. I knew I wanted to pastor, but up until that night, I don't think I'd ever given much thought to what I really wanted to see accomplished in my ministry. Was I just going to mind the store, so to speak? "Marry them and bury them," as they say? Was I just going to prepare my weekly sermons because that's what I was paid to do, or was there something else?

As the evening went on and I continued to attempt to answer Dr. Stanley's questions, our exchange caused me to think more and more about my purpose in ministry. Up until that night, I had thought about ministry in terms of what I would do: pastor a church, prepare sermons, visit people in the hospital, help the church to grow. Now his questions were forcing me to think, not so much about what I wanted to do, but what I wanted to see God do in people's lives through me.

Each question seemed to evoke another question, and Dr. Stanley never seemed to be completely satisfied with the answers I was giving him. I reached a point of almost desperation, as it appeared that my answers weren't what this man I admired so much was looking for. Finally, in almost complete desperation, I blurted out, "Dr. Stanley, I just want people to get it!"

With that, like a master teacher helping a student discover a new truth, a wry smile came across Dr. Stanley's face. He leaned back in his chair, took a sip of his iced tea, and never asked me another question the rest of the night. As we sat there, I thought, *Is that it? Is that the answer he's been looking for all night: I just want people to get it?*

I've thought about that evening a lot in the years since. I don't know what the couple who were supposed to have dinner with Dr. Stanley that night thought. It may have made them mad that he canceled on them. It may have cost his ministry financial support. I think it speaks of this man's humility and kingdom focus that he would invest an evening in my life and ministry and help me think, as I said, not so much about what I wanted to do, but what I wanted to see God do in people's lives. I am eternally grateful to Dr. Stanley, who was so willing to give so generously of his time and wisdom to a young seminary student.

"Nice story, Clay, but what's the point?" you might ask. Not long ago, I woke up in the middle of the night with those words on my mind: *I just want people to get it!* Years later the idea that Dr. Stanley birthed in my heart that night at dinner is still the driving ambition of my life. I want people to get it. I want you to get it. I want you to have in life what God promises that you can have. Money? Health? Fame? No, God has promised His children something far more valuable than temporary trinkets.

God has promised peace, purpose, joy, and contentment. He's promised power for living life to its fullest, without fear or doubt, a life without anxiety or uncertainty. It's the stuff that everybody is really looking for in life, whether they realize it or not.

> *I want to help you get it, because I know*
> *God wants you to have it.*

Jesus said, "I came that they may have life, and have it abundantly" (John 10:10). We'll get into this more in the first chapter, but if I can invade your private space for just a moment and ask you, even as we start this journey of discovery, would you say that you have life abundantly? Is it full—in a good way—and satisfying? Is it possible that you might not even know what that kind of life exactly looks like?

If so, you're not alone. In my years of ministry experience, I have met very few people who actually live the abundant life of which Jesus spoke. It's just possible that your

Introduction

picking up this book is one of those moments in your life that has the appearance of being coincidence, but may in fact be the providence of God steering you toward the life He has always meant for you.

> *You can have more. You can have better. You can have the promises of God that provide the kind of successful life that He has always intended for you to have.*

And as we'll discover in this book, it has nothing to do with how much money is in your bank account or any of the other barometers that most people use to gauge success.

The New International Version translates John 10:10 this way: "I have come that they may have life, and have it to the full" (John 10:10). In other words, to "get it." If that sounds like something you'd be interested in, read on. My prayer is that by the end of this book, you'll be able to say, *"I get it!"*

Chapter 1
What Is It?

My wife loves those singing-competition shows on television. Judging by the number of them on television, apparently a lot of people feel the same way. I admit I sit down and watch some of them with her. When you listen to the background stories of some of the contestants on these shows, a remarkable thread of consistency runs through their stories. The details vary, but many of the stories contain similar elements of difficult trials and the fact that life has been really hard.

Of course, the other element that the contestants' stories all seem to have in common is how badly they want to win the competition and how winning it all would change everything for them. But is that really true? For sure, their lives would be different. Going from standing in a high school chorus line to standing on the red carpet would be dramatically different to say the least. Going from a zip code in the middle of the Nebraska cornfields to 90210 would be a little like Dorothy landing in Oz. But would everything really be changed?

Being named the next American idol would certainly bring fame and probably a good bit of fortune, but would it bring real peace? Would it really bring lasting joy and true contentment to his or her life? Would it eliminate stress, anxiety, fear, worry, and any number of other negative emotions that most people experience in life, whether they can sing or not?

Sadly, stories from *Extra* and other such shows that keep us in the know about those we love to know about would say no. Statistically speaking, people with money, power, and fame aren't any more content than the average person. They have a higher rate of divorce, a greater degree of drug dependency, and are generally no more contented in life. They have nicer toys than most of us, but that doesn't necessarily translate into a nicer life.

So what's my point? Just this:

> *What if the lack of true peace and contentment in life runs much deeper than the size of your paycheck, the square footage of your house, the emblem on your car, or the label on your clothes? What if the answer to what really brings true meaning, purpose, and joy to life is not physical, but spiritual?*

Since this book is about God and His promises, you can probably guess what I think. But if I'm right, it means that millions of people in our culture have run down the rabbit hole of materialism in search of a wonderland of contentment, meaning, and purpose where there is no fear or anxiety, and they've ended up wondering why they still aren't happy, satisfied, or at peace in their lives.

Just to be clear, let me turn the question I asked earlier into a declarative statement: the answer to what really brings true meaning, purpose, and joy to life is not physical, but spiritual. None other than the creator of the universe—aka God—promises it to you!

You may have picked up this book and you consider yourself a person of faith, or you may have picked it up and you don't consider yourself a very spiritual person at all. Maybe you've figured out that the way you're doing life now isn't really working, but you're not ready to sell everything you own and go join a monastery. Me either! Nor do I think we have to in order to experience the promises of God.

The problem is that there seems to be a great deal of confusion about what makes for a spiritual life. Wilbur Rees has captured well the spiritual condition of a lot of people when he writes:

> I would like to buy $3 worth of God, please. Not enough to explode my soul or disturb my sleep, but just enough to equal a cup of warm milk or a snooze in the sunshine. I don't want enough of Him to make me love a black man or pick beets with a migrant. I want ecstasy, not transformation; I want the warmth of the womb, not a new birth. I want a pound of the Eternal in a paper sack. I would like to buy $3 worth of God, please.[1]

Is that it? Is that what God intended for us, a faith that is equivalent to "a cup of warm milk" or a "snooze in the sunshine"? Is "Christian" simply a religious status on our Facebook profile that really has little bearing on our daily lives? Is it something to make us feel better about ourselves along the way and to bring some sense of security about where we will spend eternity, but doesn't really impact our here and now? Or is it possible that Jesus had something else in mind when He said, "I came to give life—life in all its fullness" (John 10:10 NCV).

The truth is, I meet a lot of people who seem to sense that something is missing in their relationship with God. Through my years in ministry, I've encountered many men and women who, at some point in their journey through life, have become frustrated with what they rightfully perceive as a disconnect between the type of life and faith that they read about in the Bible and what their lives look like on a daily basis. Even if you've never given much thought to a relationship with God and have never read the Bible, you may very well have a sense of dissatisfaction with the way things are in your life.

Of course, none of us who are followers of Jesus (we'll talk more about that later) ever intended for it to be this way. When we came to faith in Christ, it was with a heart full of gratitude to God for choosing to love us and with a genuine desire to please God with our lives. We had this idea that following Jesus was going to be exciting, fulfilling, and rewarding. And we couldn't wait to get started on this journey with God! And for many of us there was an expectation—although a naïve one—that it was going to be easy.

But a funny thing happened along the way. We ran into life—not the one we were hoping for, where the sun always shines on us, the sky is always blue for us, and the birds always sing to us; but the one that brought with it pressure, responsibility, bills, drama, relational struggles, emotional baggage, trials, fears, hardships, and all the other stuff that can make life so tough. Everybody went looking for Pleasantville, but a lot people feel like they took a wrong turn somewhere and ended up in Amityville.

In fact, maybe in the craziness of your life, Jesus' words "I have come that they may have life, and have it to the full" (John 10:10 NIV) have all but disappeared. If you got real honest and you knew your mom wouldn't hear it, you might be tempted to say, "Life is full of something all right, and it stinks!"

What Is It?

If that's how you feel, then I say, "That's great!" Sorry, I don't mean to sound giddy over the difficult circumstances of your life, but knowing that something in your spiritual walk with God isn't right is half the battle. Okay, maybe not half, but it is really important because just maybe it means (I apologize in advance for using old worn-out clichés) you're sick and tired of being sick and tired.

When I was in seminary, I went on my first international mission trip. I was doing work with a local church in a small village in western Kenya near the Ugandan border. A man in a nearby village had died, and the village was holding his funeral. When I say the village was holding his funeral, that's exactly what I mean. Everyone turned out to grieve with the family. The pastor said it would honor the family if we went and paid our respects.

As we walked along the narrow dirt path that led to the village, the pastor said rather casually, "You will speak at the funeral." I quickly looked around to see who had joined us on that little sunbaked piece of the African landscape, because he couldn't possibly be talking to me! *I'm just a seminary student! I don't speak the language! I don't know the man who died! I don't have an outline!*

I'm sure the pastor saw the panic-stricken look on my face as I looked over at him because he said reassuringly, "The family, they will want you to speak at the funeral." Suddenly my mind was racing a million miles an hour. The pastor had already mentioned that the man who had died was not a follower of Jesus. What could I possibly say that would offer any hope or encouragement to this family?

Sure enough, by the time we arrived, the entire village had gathered and was waiting for us to get there. Apparently, word had already spread that the American would be speaking at the funeral. As we entered the village a strange silence came over the crowd gathered there. All eyes were on us and the crowd cleared a path as we made our way through the people and stopped in front of the deceased man's thatched-roof hut. It was like a scene from some movie, only I was in it!

It seems that the plan was for me to speak and the local pastor would translate. After what seemed like a rather lengthy introduction, the pastor gave me a nod that it was my time to speak. I opened my Bible and read from the book of Ecclesiastes:

For everything there is a season, a time for every activity under heaven.
A time to be born and a time to die.
A time to plant and a time to harvest.
A time to kill and a time to heal.
A time to tear down and a time to build up.
A time to cry and a time to laugh.
A time to grieve and a time to dance.
A time to scatter stones and a time to gather stones.
A time to embrace and a time to turn away.
A time to search and a time to quit searching.
A time to keep and a time to throw away.
A time to tear and a time to mend.
A time to be quiet and a time to speak.
A time to love and a time to hate.
A time for war and a time for peace.
—Ecclesiastes 3:1–8

I went on to talk about the brevity of life and the certainty of death. I explained that it didn't matter if you lived in Africa or America; time passes faster than we realize. I described what the Bible teaches about what gives real value to life and how we could have eternal life. I described the difference that having a relationship with Jesus can make in our lives. I have no idea how the Lord used what I said, but the pastor seemed pleased.

That passage in Ecclesiastes is perhaps one of the most introspective in the Bible. When we read it, if we are real with ourselves, it forces us to take stock of our own lives and to evaluate whether we are really getting out of life all that the Bible promises we can have. For instance, I know I keep bringing this verse up, but Jesus said in John chapter 10: "I came that they may have life, and have it abundantly" (John 10:10). Another translation puts it this way: "I have come that they may have life, and have it to the full" (John 10:10 NIV). I kind of like the way the New Living Translation puts that verse: "My purpose is to give them a rich and satisfying life" (John 10:10 NLT).

Let's be honest; would adjectives like "rich" and "satisfying" describe your life? Would you say you have life "abundantly"? Are you living it "to the full"? If you are, that's great! But sadly, the majority of people I meet, if asked, would say (and remember, we're being honest), "None of those words describe my life!" Well, they might say it's full, but full of stress, anxiety, worry, fear, depression, doubt, disappointment, and a whole host of other things that make life anything but satisfying or abundant.

Or how about this one? "Peace I leave with you; My peace I give to you; not as the world gives do I give to you. Do not let your heart be troubled, nor let it be fearful" (John 14:27). Would *peace* characterize your life even in the midst of the stuff life throws at you? Is your heart untroubled and free of fear?

What about all the promises of *joy*? The psalmist said, "But let all who take refuge in You be glad, let them ever sing for joy; and may You shelter them, that those who love Your name may exult in You" (Psalm 5:11). In Psalm 16, we read, "You will make known to me the path of life; in Your presence is fullness of joy; in Your right hand there are pleasures forever" (Psalm 16:11).

Jesus had a little something to say about joy as well: "These things I have spoken to you so that My joy may be in you, and that your joy may be made full" (John 15:11). Would you say His joy is in you? Would you say that you experience the fullness of joy in your life on a daily basis?

What about *hope*? That's another good word. The apostle Paul wrote to the church in Rome and said, "Now may the God of hope fill you with all joy and peace in believing, so that you will abound in hope by the power of the Holy Spirit" (Romans 15:13). Again, would you say that you "abound in hope"? Do you have "all joy and peace"?

What about *contentment*? Again, Paul writes while in a prison cell, "Not that I was ever in need, for I have learned how to be content with whatever I have. I know how to live on almost nothing or with everything. I have learned the secret of living in every situation, whether it is with a full stomach or empty, with plenty or little" (Philippians 4:11–12 NLT).

What an unbelievable statement! What would it be like to be able to say, "I have learned to be content with whatever I have"? Good times or bad times, health or sickness, great boss or a bad boss, strong financial portfolio or living paycheck to paycheck, "I have learned to be content with whatever life throws at me." What would that kind of contentment in life be worth to you? Like the credit card commercial says: "Priceless."

Over and over again, God's Word promises a satisfying, abundant life with characteristics like peace, joy, and contentment as an everyday part of life. So here's the million-dollar question:

> *If God says that kind of life is what we can have, should have, and that He wants us to have, then why don't people have it? Why don't you have it?*

Why are so many people experiencing so very little of the kind of life that the Bible says that they can and should have? After more than twenty years in ministry and after being an eyewitness to countless crises in men and women's lives, I think I can safely say that there is a major disconnect between the promises of God and the reality of His children's lives.

The truth is, many people go to church, sing the songs, maybe even lift their hands in praise; they pray the prayers, listen to the messages, nod in agreement, voice their amens, and talk at lunch about how good church was today. Then Monday comes, and they go back to their daily lives where God's promises of power and peace and joy and contentment seem like nothing more than a spiritual pipe dream. To most people, the promises of God sound great in theory, look great on paper, but are so far removed from their real-world, real-life experience that they can't even imagine what it would be like to actually live in those promises on a daily basis.

I've always enjoyed Steven Curtis Chapman's music. To me, his songs capture much of what a life in Christ should be like. One of my favorite of his songs is titled "More to This Life." The chorus sums it up best:

> But there's more to this life than living and dying,
>
> More than just trying to make it through the day.
>
> More to this life, more than these eyes alone can see,
>
> And there's more than this life alone can be.[2]

Those words get to the heart of what all of us have felt at one time or another, both Christians and non-Christians, and that is that there has to be more to life than just existing.

Surely we're not just marking time until our number is called. I believe that deep within the heart of every one of us is the God-given understanding that life is meant to be more than just endured. God intends for life to be enjoyed!

As I've already stated, our culture, for the most part, teaches us that the answer is found in the accumulation of stuff. We're taught to live by the adage "Get all you can, while you can, for as long as you can, until you kick the can!" Happiness is found in possessions, power, parties, and popularity. Buy a bigger house, drive a nicer car, find a new relationship, climb higher on the corporate ladder, and then you'll finally be content. It is the "he who dies with the most toys wins" mentality.

Even well-meaning parents contribute to this philosophy of happiness through accumulation when they tell their kids things like, "You've got to get good grades so that you can go to a good college so that you can get a good job so that you can make a good living, live in a good neighborhood, and afford the good things in life." Translation: The "good" life consists of accumulating stuff.

I'm certainly not proposing that we teach our kids that good grades aren't important. The problem, which we'll discuss more fully in the next chapter, is that everybody knows, or should know, that trying to find real peace, joy, and contentment in the accumulation of stuff simply doesn't work. Owners of storage facilities may be getting rich renting storage units to people looking for a place to keep all their stuff, but we aren't getting any closer to contentment by having all that stuff.

Even people without any regard for what God can do for them seem to know from experience that the "stuff" of life never really brings any true lasting fulfillment or satisfaction. At best, it dulls the pain for a short period of time until the luster wears off and the warranty runs out and they're forced to try to get their "happy fix" in something or someone else.

Of course, followers of Jesus know it as well. We not only know it practically, but we know it prophetically. God's Word is clear that the things of this world will never bring the peace, joy, and contentment that everyone is ultimately looking for in life. Jesus told us that when He said: "Beware, and be on your guard against every form of greed; for not even when one has an abundance does his life consist of his possessions" (Luke 12:15).

So how do we take hold of the promises of God's Word and make them a reality in our lives? How do we actually live an abundant, satisfying, full life filled with peace, joy, and contentment? How do we learn to let go of our stress, anxieties, fears, and doubts and take hold of the promises of God?

As I stood in front of that mud-and-manure, thatched-roof hut that hot, muggy day in Kenya, I reminded the people in that little village that God's Word tells us, "For everything there is a season, a time for every activity under heaven" (Ecclesiastes 3:1). The season of abundant living is now. It's time for you to have the life that God intends for you to have. Are you ready? Turn the page and let's see if we can discover how to really get it!

Chapter 2

Why Don't I Have It?

I grew up on a farm. It was fun being the son of a dairy farmer. My dad made sure his sons did their share of work, washing out the barn, bailing hay, sweeping the feed room, and other things that go with farm living. It was hard work, but there was also plenty of time to be a kid.

When I was about six years old, one of my favorite places in the barn was what was known as the cooler room. It was where the milk was stored in giant refrigeration tanks until it was taken to the processing plant. The pipes leading into the tanks were always frozen over with a thick coating of ice. The pipes were all white and crystallized, and the ice glistened and sparkled in the light. And it looked delicious to a six-year-old!

By now, you've probably guessed what happened. No one was in the cooler room as I walked in one day. Those glistening, sparkling, delicious-looking frozen pipes appeared to me like the greatest thing since, well, like the greatest thing ever! (Remember, I was six.) It was like those frozen pipes were calling to me, beckoning me to come give them a try.

So I leaned over and touched my tongue to the ice-encased pipe with every expectation that this was going to be great. But it didn't quite turn out the way I expected. Just like that kid in the movie *A Christmas Story,* my tongue instantly froze to the pipe. I didn't know what to do except scream as loud as I could. It's hard to yell "help" when you've got a pipe stuck to your tongue. Trust me on this.

After what seemed like an eternity (time moves much more slowly in a situation like that), the foreman of the dairy came running into the room. All he could see was his boss's youngest son on his knees, back turned towards him, arms flailing wildly in the air, with unintelligible words coming out of his mouth. I don't know if he thought I was hurt or was having a Pentecostal moment, but he ran over to me, grabbed me by the shoulders (you may want to turn away at this point), and yanked. I came loose, but the top layer of skin on my tongue didn't. To this day, I have a fear of popsicles!

You know, that wasn't at all what I had envisioned when I walked into that cooler room that day. The ice around that pipe looked so inviting and delicious. I just knew it was going to taste sweet and be the best thing I'd ever had. But the experience was very different from the expectation.

The same is often true when a person comes to faith in Jesus Christ. I said in the last chapter that as followers of Jesus, we usually know when something's not right in our Christian lives. You don't have to be a Bible scholar or even the son or daughter of a Bible scholar to recognize that for a large number of Christians, there's a discrepancy between what the Bible teaches about the way their lives should look and the way they actually are. Their Christian experience doesn't match up to the expectation they had when they made the decision to follow Christ.

Having said that, however, it's amazing how easy it is to settle into our version of the Christian life. And that's the first part of the problem as to why we don't have the life that God says that we can have.

Bad Programming

We rationalize the glaring differences between our lives and the lives of God's people in Scripture by putting them on a spiritual pedestal. Here's what I mean. We look at biblical characters like Moses, Abraham, Esther, Mary, Paul, and others, and we say, "Wow, what amazing believers they were! I could never have the faith to follow God to a place I'd never been before and leave practically everything I'd ever known behind like Abraham did. I could never put my life on the line like Queen Esther did. I could never believe God like Mary did. I could never have joy in the middle of trials like Paul did."

In short, we make the men and women of the Bible, and even a handful of people we may know personally, spiritual supermen and superwomen. We feel we're just as saved as they are. We're confident we'll be in heaven with them, but they just seem to have a little something extra that we don't. God obviously must have touched them in a special way.

Now let's see. What's that ancient Hebrew word I'm looking for? Oh yeah — *baloney*! That may not sound very spiritual, but it's the best word I can think of to describe the faulty programming that many followers of Jesus have. And it's keeping them from living in the promises of God!

The men and women that we read about in the Bible weren't spiritual supermen and superwomen. They had struggles. They had doubts and fears. They even had failings. The same is true for the few men and women we may know today who are actually living out the promises of God. They haven't been touched in a special way or given an extra dose of the Holy Spirit to help them succeed when others seem to struggle along in their faith.

It seems that a lot of people have been programmed to believe that there is some type of class system in Christianity, with the spiritual giants at the top of the food chain enjoying all the promises of God—joy, peace, contentment, etc.—and the rest of us "normal" Christians just struggling to keep it together another day while we wait for Jesus to come back and take us out of all this mess. Let me say it again—baloney!

How this bad programming came to be a part of our thinking is hard to say, and maybe it doesn't even matter. What matters is that you understand that the people that you read about in the Bible, and the ones that you know who seem to get it, aren't any different from you, except that they've discovered how to really live in the promises of God.

Bad Perspective

Not only have too many followers of Jesus had bad programming, but there's also a problem with a bad perspective. We're focused way too much on the temporal and not nearly enough on the eternal. Be honest. During the course of an average day, how often do you think about your circumstances from God's perspective? If you're like most people, the thought of God's perspective rarely enters your mind.

A temporal perspective tells us that we can't be content unless our circumstances are good. If our bills are all paid, if our kids are healthy, if our job is smooth, and if our life is free of stress, then everything's good. Then we're "happy."

Now never mind that good circumstances don't equate to contentment or happiness anyway, but does the description I just gave really fit anybody's life that you know? Because I sure don't know of anybody who has a life totally free of problems and adversity. Let's face it; in the real game of life, nobody gets to "pass go and collect two hundred dollars" every time around the board.

Most of the people I know have lives where their circumstances are anything but ideal. Money gets tight sometimes (maybe most times) for a lot of us. Health issues can vary from minor to major. Jobs can be demanding. Relationships can be rocky, and stress is as common as One Direction downloads at a teenage girls' sleepover.

That's the life that most of us live with every day, and it's easy for our circumstances to skew our perspective. Now contrast that with the apostle Paul's perspective when he wrote: "I have learned how to be content with whatever I have. I know how to live on almost nothing or with everything. I have learned the secret of living in every situation, whether it is with a full stomach or empty, with plenty or little. For I can do everything through Christ, who gives me strength" (Philippians 4:11–13 NLT).

Were Paul's circumstances easier than ours? No. As a matter of fact, Paul experienced more trials, adversity, and hardships in his life than most of us can even imagine, or will ever have to endure. I can hear it now: "See there! You've just proven my point. Paul was a spiritual superman!" No, Paul wasn't a spiritual superman. Paul was a spiritual in-tune man. Instead of being tuned in to or focused on his circumstances, Paul was tuned in to something far more important. Paul had the right perspective, an eternal one, and because he did, his peace, joy, and contentment weren't held hostage by his circumstances.

Here's the way Paul explained it: "Since you have been raised to new life with Christ, set your sights on the realities of heaven, where Christ sits in the place of honor at God's right hand. Think about the things of heaven, not the things of earth. For you died to this life, and your real life is hidden with Christ in God. And when Christ, who is your life, is revealed to the whole world, you will share in all his glory" (Colossians 3:1–4 NLT).

Have you ever seen one of those pictures that just look like a bunch of dots? When you first look at it, all you can see are those dots, but if you get right up to it and stare at it long enough, a totally different picture emerges. What changed the picture? The difference was your focus. When your focus changed, then you suddenly had a whole new perspective of the picture that was in front of you. The same is true in our daily lives. When we begin to change our focus from our circumstances to God's promises, from the temporal to the eternal, that's when our whole perspective begins to change. And that's when we begin to get it!

"Okay, you've got me listening. So how do I get the right perspective?" Well, for one thing, you first have to recognize that there's a problem, and that's what this chapter is all about. We'll start getting to the answer in the next chapter, but for now, let's look at another part of the problem.

Bad Preparation

My wife, Cindi, and I have a friend named Kelley. She's a world-class pianist, a graduate of Julliard and extremely accomplished in her field. I was talking with Kelley one day about performing. I was shocked when she told me that she spends approximately six hours a day, pretty much every day of her life, practicing the piano. Sure, I knew that you have to continue to practice some, but I just assumed that once you reached a certain level of proficiency, you only had to really prepare just before a performance. I'll never forget what Kelley said to me: "Clay, if I only prepare when I'm going to give a performance, I won't be prepared to give the performance."

Followers of Jesus often seem to have the idea about their spiritual lives that I did about piano performances: the only time they really have to prepare is when something big is going on. Here's the thing though, all of life is big! There are always relational issues or health issues or financial issues or job issues or a thousand other issues going on at any given time in our lives. And most of the Christians I meet just aren't prepared. They are just as stressed out, burnt out, and wrung out as the people who don't follow Jesus.

One day I was walking through the living room, and the television was on. The conversation on the show caused me to stop. I saw that a soap-opera family was in a crisis. (I know, right? Hard to believe someone on a soap opera was in crisis.) Anyway, the family was all gathered together for a meal, and before they ate, the patriarch of the family said, "I think we should pray [organ music, dramatic pause]. If ever we needed God, it's now."

It may have been a soap opera, and soap operas are usually about as real as a Sasquatch sighting, but I can tell you from years of ministry experience, that family patriarch's mind-set is the mind-set of a lot of people in the real world. What I mean is this: for too many people, God is like the spare tire in the trunk of their car. It's comforting to know that He's there if they need Him, but otherwise, they don't really give much thought to Him.

News flash! God is not a magic genie that we can summon out of the bottle to come and grant our wish and make everything right. He's Lord, and He's given us what we need to live in the reality of His promises. But there has to be personal preparation on our part, or we will never live in the reality of God's promises.

So if we aren't properly prepared, we just won't be ready for the stuff life throws at us. And we've already established—and I don't think anyone would argue—that life is going to throw stuff at us. Like a major league fastball, the circumstances of life are coming at you and me at near triple digits. But remember, God doesn't just want us to have a chance to duck and get out of the way. He wants us to knock it out of the ballpark! God doesn't want us to just survive our circumstances. He wants us to thrive in our circumstances!

So bad programming, bad perspective, and bad preparation are a big part of the problem for people trying to live in the promises of God. However, there's another threefold part of the problem that is equally important to consider before we move on.

The Devil Deceives

Our enemy is known by many names: Abaddon, which in Hebrew means "destruction," Beelzebub, Lucifer, Satan, and of course, the devil. The apostle Peter reminds us, "Your enemy the devil prowls around like a roaring lion looking for someone to devour" (1 Peter 5:8 NIV). Jesus said, "The thief comes only to steal and kill and destroy" (John 10:10).

Earlier in this chapter, I asked the question, how often do you think about your circumstances from God's perspective? Let me ask another question: how often do you think about the fact that there is someone out there who wants to destroy you? Again, if you are like most people, you'd probably say, "Not very often."

It's not like we haven't been warned. Over and over again, we read on the pages of God's Word of the devil's exploits. Time and time again, God tells us of Satan's treachery and hatred for God's children. So how is it that all too often we walk into the battle with little or no preparation against an enemy who is seeking to steal our contentment, kill our joy, and destroy our peace? How can we be so unprepared for an enemy who wants to strip us of all the promises of God and leave us with a life sorely lacking God's power? I'm afraid too often we underestimate our enemy and overestimate our ability to handle what he brings against us.

One of the main strategies the enemy employs is one that he has used since the beginning. Jesus said this about the devil: "He was a murderer from the beginning, and does not stand in the truth because there is no truth in him. Whenever he speaks a lie, he speaks from his own nature, for he is a liar and the father of lies" (John 8:44). All the way back in the Garden of Eden, the devil came to Adam and Eve and deceived them into thinking they'd be better off disregarding God's warning and rebelling against His command not to eat of the fruit from the tree of the knowledge of good and evil:

> Now the serpent was more crafty than any beast of the field which the Lord God had made. And he said to the woman, "Indeed, has God said, 'You shall not eat from any tree of the garden'?" The woman said to the serpent, "From the fruit of the trees of the garden we may eat; but from the fruit of the tree which is in the middle of the garden, God has said, 'You shall not eat from it or touch it, or you will die.' " The serpent said to the woman, "You surely will not die! For God knows that in the day you eat from it your eyes will be opened, and you will be like God, knowing good and evil." —Genesis 3:1–5

Notice Satan's attack on both the integrity of God's nature and the authority of God's word. Satan convinced Eve that God didn't have Adam and Eve's best interests at heart, that God was really trying to keep them down. Satan even told them that they wouldn't really die, even though God had declared that they would.

Sadly, Eve bought the lie, bit the fruit, and bore the consequences.

The devil's strategy really hasn't changed from that time to today. Many people I meet have been deceived into thinking that God's Word is not authoritative and is irrelevant for their lives and that they don't need God to be happy. So they go off trying to find happiness in anything and everything else, and they end up disappointed and disillusioned.

The Culture Distracts

We live in a culture where entertainment is king. From movies and music, theme parks and cruise ships, gaming, reality TV, and the World Wide Web, there are countless ways for us to amuse ourselves these days.

That's not to say that those things are in themselves bad. But how easy it is to become distracted by what culture has to offer us and lose sight of what God has for our lives. In fact, one of the reasons we aren't prepared for the attacks from our enemy is because we're too distracted by the things that the world has to offer.

At one time in my life, I was an aspiring tennis player. I was seeking a top ten state ranking. I loved it. I not only loved it, but I also lived it. Two to three hours a day, I was on the court, practicing, traveling to tournaments, watching matches on television, reading articles in tennis magazines. I was a follower of Jesus at that point in my life. I was in church pretty much every Sunday. But I was missing the life God had intended for me.

Is tennis wrong? No. Are having goals and trying to reach levels wrong? Certainly not. But when the things in this world distract us and keep us from becoming the followers of Jesus we were meant to be, then something has gotten off track.

So the devil seeks to deceive us, and the culture tries to distract us. Those two working together can make it extremely difficult for us. But there is one more problem we have to recognize and come to grips with.

The Flesh Desires

We are a people consumed with consumerism. If we don't have it, we want it. If our neighbor already has it, then we want the newer, bigger model. Materialism is the drug of choice for most of us. Our flesh cries out:

> *"I want what I want, when I want it, and if I don't get it, I can't possibly be happy!"*

It's the pull of our flesh. Whether it's a bigger house, a newer car, another relationship, or whatever, our flesh craves it. Not surprisingly, the Bible has something to say about the pull of the flesh and its consequences:

> Those who live according to the flesh have their minds set on what the flesh desires; but those who live in accordance with the Spirit have their minds set on what the Spirit desires. The mind governed by the flesh is death, but the mind governed by the Spirit is life and peace.—Romans 8:5–6 NIV

> For the flesh desires what is contrary to the Spirit, and the Spirit what is contrary to the flesh. They are in conflict with each other, so that you are not to do whatever you want.
> —Galatians 5:17 NIV

> All of us also lived among them at one time, gratifying the cravings of our flesh and following its desires and thoughts. Like the rest, we were by nature deserving of wrath.
> —Ephesians 2:3 NIV

So bad programming, bad perspective, and bad preparation, along with a deceiving enemy, a distracting culture, and the desires of our flesh, all work together to work against us and keep us from experiencing the life God intended for us. We want peace of mind and heart, but instead we often end up with anxiety and strife. We want contentment in our lives, but instead we have dissatisfaction and restlessness. We want hope, but instead we feel hopeless. We want security, but instead we experience fear and uncertainty. Surely that's not the life God intended for His children. Surely there's something better for us if we just knew how to get it.

Good news! There is something better. There is "life more abundant," as Jesus promised. So let's get to it. Turn the page and begin to discover the prescription.

Chapter 3

Do I Really Want It?

This chapter's title may seem a little odd to you because you've invested the money to buy this book (my family thanks you) and you're investing the time to read it. So it certainly appears that you want to "get it." And I'm sure you do, but I'm also sure, at least for some of you, that there may be a part of you that just doesn't really think that it can happen for you. Let me try to explain what I mean.

If you were sick and someone asked you, "Do you want to get better?" you would think that a strange question, wouldn't you? It certainly must have seemed strange to the paralyzed man in John chapter 5, but that's exactly the question Jesus asked him.

There was a pool in Jerusalem that had come to be known as a healing place. John tells us that many people believed that at certain times of the year, an angel would come down and stir the water in the pool. Tradition said that the first person to get into the pool after the angel stirred the water would be healed of any sickness or infirmity.

John doesn't tell us whether the tradition was true or not, just that the people believed it to be. As you can imagine, that pool had become quite a gathering place for the sick, the blind, and the lame.

"One who was there had been an invalid for thirty-eight years. When Jesus saw him lying there and learned that he had been in this condition for a long time, he asked him, 'Do you want to get well?' " (John 5:5–6 NIV).

Like I said, what a strange question to ask a person who can't walk. Of course he wanted to get well! He wanted to walk and run and jump. He wanted to stand on his own two feet, figuratively and literally. He wanted to enjoy life without the shackles of a handicap that left him a prisoner to a ragged, worn-out piece of carpet and at the mercy of others' pity. Why would Jesus ask a question that had such an obvious answer? Well, maybe the answer is not quite as obvious as you and I might think. Look at the paralyzed man's response to Jesus' question: " 'Sir,' the invalid replied, 'I have no one to help me into the pool when the water is stirred. While I am trying to get in, someone else goes down ahead of me' " (John 5:7 NIV).

Thirty-eight years this man had been in this condition—certainly the majority, if not all, of his life. How long he had been at the pool, we don't know, but the implication is he'd been there a long time. We don't know how he got to the pool in the first place. Did friends or family bring him there? Did he crawl there under his own power? No doubt, when he first arrived at the pool known as Bethesda, he had high hopes of being healed. But his response to Jesus reveals that an even worse condition than his paralysis had set in. This man had lost hope.

Yes, no doubt, the man wanted to be healed, and certainly Jesus knew that, but the paralyzed man had lost all hope of ever being healed. Experience had taught him that he was never going to be the first one into the pool, so he was never going to get well. So there he lay, day after day, eating the dust from the crowds as they, and life, passed him by. He was perhaps only a few feet from freedom, but as far as that man was concerned, it might as well have been a million miles. The reason was because the paralytic no longer possessed the physical strength to get into the water, and apparently, no one else was willing to help him. Worst of all, he no longer possessed the hope to even try. This was just the life he was going to have.

Earlier we looked at some of the promises of God concerning the kind of life we can have. It is a wonderful life filled with purpose and peace, joy and security, satisfaction and contentment. Of course, everyone wants that kind of life. I've never met anybody who said to me, "I want to be miserable. I like being anxious. I want to live in fear with no purpose or joy or peace in my life—and don't you dare try to change it!"

No, we all want abundant living. But is it possible that like the paralyzed man on the mat, you've lost all hope of ever having the kind of life Jesus promised? Have you become a prisoner to a life of stress, anxiety, and hopelessness the way that man was a prisoner of the mat he lived his life on? In a very real way, are you just as paralyzed as that man by the pool, unable to get up and move forward in the life God's Word has promised, void of the hope of it ever changing, and resigning yourself to the fact that this is just the life you're going to have? Then maybe this is a good time to ask Jesus' question again:

Do you want to get well?

Do you want to hope again that God will give you what His Word promises He can give you? Are you willing to believe that God really can cause you to rise up and walk in abundant life? If so, then congratulations! You've actually taken the first step (pun intended) toward filling the prescription to have the kind of life that God wants you to have.

You Have to Hope Again

Now, as followers of Jesus, it's important to understand that godly hope is not the same thing as worldly hope. When I was a kid, I "hoped" that I would someday be a star in the NBA. I would shoot baskets for hours and pretend I was some basketball great making the game-winning shot. But the truth was, I had neither the physical attributes nor the skill set that would ever allow me to see that hope become a reality. I could continue to work hard, and I could get better as a basketball player, to some degree. But I was never going to be any taller than five eleven, I wasn't going to get any faster than middle of the pack, and with a vertical leap that allowed me to easily clear a small dog, I was never going to have what it takes to get to the big show. In fact, my hope was nothing more than wishful thinking, and that's no hope at all. The truth is, I just didn't have what I needed.

That's the great thing about godly hope: we already have exactly what we need for the kind of life we all hope to have! If you've entered into a personal relationship with Jesus Christ, then God the Holy Spirit dwells within you, and the Bible says, "Children, you belong to God, and you have defeated these enemies. God's Spirit is in you and is more powerful than the one that is in the world" (1 John 4:4 CEV).

Isn't that exciting? God not only gives you the promise of abundant living, but He also gives you the power to have it! We'll talk more about the role of the Holy Spirit later, but for now, take hope in the fact that living in the promises of God isn't just wishful thinking. It can be a reality. And when looking for the prescription for abundant living, keep the following in mind as well:

You Have to Get the Prescription from the Right Source

That may seem like a no-brainer, but it's not as easy as you might think. People love to give advice. Almost everybody has an opinion or idea or philosophy or teaching that they've come across that promises to be the key to a happy life. It might be Oprah, Dr. Phil, Dr. Oz, a life coach (what is that, anyway?), your mother-in-law, or a hundred other so-called experts. They may be sincere in their beliefs, but they can still be sincerely wrong.

At this point, you might be tempted to say, "But isn't that exactly what you're doing? Aren't you claiming to have the prescription for a rich, rewarding, complete life?" Yes, I am, but the difference is, I'm right and they're wrong! I'm just kidding, sort of. I do believe I have the answer, but it's not based on any man-made philosophy or self-help book. It's based on the Word of God.

The writer of the book of Hebrews reminds us: "For the word of God is alive and active. Sharper than any double-edged sword, it penetrates even to dividing soul and spirit, joints and marrow; it judges the thoughts and attitudes of the heart" (Hebrews 4:12 NIV). The Word of God has the power to surgically remove from our lives things that don't belong: sin, fear, stress, anger, and all the other stuff that robs us of the life God wants us to have. At the same time, the Word of God has the power to surgically "sew" into our lives the things that do belong: joy, love, peace, contentment, and all the other promises that God has given to us and that everyone wants.

We'll get to the specifics of the prescription in the coming chapters, but let me share one more piece of counsel regarding the prescription:

You Have to Use as Directed

The most effective prescription in the world is useless unless taken as directed. Suppose someone discovered a cure for all cancers, and doctors began to prescribe this new wonder drug that would completely destroy cancer cells in a person's body. The prescription would include very specific instructions as to how much of the drug to take, how often, and for how long. Let me ask you a question: if you had cancer, can you imagine any scenario where you wouldn't take the prescription exactly as directed? The answer is an emphatic no! You'd read, reread and probably re-reread those directions to make sure you knew exactly what you were supposed to do.

If it was a pill and it said to take it with milk, you'd stockpile milk in your fridge to make sure you had what you needed. If it said to take it at 2:07 in the morning, you'd set three alarm clocks and be up by 1:45 waiting for the precise moment as prescribed. If the prescription said to take it standing on one leg on top of the Empire State Building, you'd be booking your flight to the Big Apple yesterday!

The reason you'd follow the prescription so precisely and completely is because the quality of your life would be directly impacted by your willingness to use the prescription as directed.

With that in mind, let me ask you another question: if God has a prescription for abundant life that will directly impact the quality of not only your physical life, but your spiritual, eternal life as well, doesn't it make even more sense to use His prescription exactly as directed?

So if you would dare to hope again that God really will give you the kind of life that His Word promises, and you're willing to get the prescription from the right source, and you'll use that prescription as directed, then you're well on your way to getting it. Exactly what is the prescription? That's what the next three chapters are all about. Keep going. You're getting it!

Chapter 4

Where Does It Come From?

When I was in high school, I was a member of the local chapter of the Future Farmers of America. I don't know that I had any intention of being a farmer in the future, but I had every intention of owning one of those stylish blue corduroy jackets! Okay, the fashion police would probably arrest me for that last statement, but as I mentioned earlier, I grew up on a dairy farm and went to school in a farming town, and being a part of FFA, well, that just went along with the territory.

Being in FFA meant I had certain agricultural-type classes I had to take, one of which was agricultural mechanics. My teacher for that class was affectionately known to us as "Sparky." Mr. Clark got his nickname as a result of an unfortunate accident that occurred in class one day. I won't go into the details, but let's just say it involved a screwdriver and a wall socket. You can probably guess what happened.

One year, as a class project, Mr. Clark had us help him build a competition tractor for tractor pulls. If you were raised in the country, you probably already know what that is. But for those who may be agriculturally challenged, a tractor pull is where someone drives a souped-up tractor, pulling a weighted sled down a dirt track as far and as fast as he can. I admit, to the uninitiated urbanite, this ritual may seem strange, even bizarre; but when you live in the country, anything that involves a lot of horsepower, a lot of noise, and a lot of dirt is usually a big hit!

I'll never forget the first time 'Sparky' decided to take his tractor out for a test run. We knew this was going to get good when we saw fire shoot from the exhaust headers as he started up the engine. Fire coming out of upturned exhaust pipes can be quite intoxicating for high school boys, you know.

He slowly idled the tractor onto the long dirt road in front of the shop-class building. Have you ever seen a jet fighter sitting on the deck of an aircraft carrier just before it's catapulted off? This was like that, only without wings or a helmet.

As he hit the accelerator, fire once more shot out of the exhaust pipes. The front end leapt into the air like a cobra preparing to strike. The roar of the engine was deafening. Sparky held on for dear life as his homemade hot-rod tractor went screaming down the road like the Millennium Falcon making the jump to hyperspace.

When he finally brought the steel beast to a stop and turned off the engine, there was a moment of complete and total silence. Even the birds seemed stunned into silence. As the remnants of smoke from the fire-breathing beast drifted off into the distance, not a single word was spoken. None were needed. Mr. Clark's ashen face and windswept hair told the story that words never could: Sparky had way more power than he realized.

Would you believe me if I told you that you already have way more power than you realize to live in the promises of God?

Where Does It Come From?

If you have a personal relationship with God (we'll discuss that further in the next chapter), then you already possess all the power you will ever need to live the life God intends for you. Let me say that again because it's that important: if you have a personal relationship with God, you already possess all the power you will ever need to live the life God intends for you to live. That power has a name—and His name is the Holy Spirit.

Almost seventeen hundred years ago, the Orthodox Church came to a proper theological understanding of who the Holy Spirit is, rightfully declaring Him a part of the triune Godhead, coequal and coeternal with God the Father and God the Son. Practically speaking, though, the role of the Holy Spirit in believers' lives has often been misunderstood or, perhaps worse, completely ignored.

As I mentioned a moment ago, the Orthodox Church came to that position officially in AD 325 at what is known as the Council of Nicaea. Constantine, the Roman emperor, had called for the council to settle a theological controversy that centered on Jesus' relationship to God the Father. The result was a document that came to be known as the Nicene Creed. That document articulated a theological understanding of one God made up of three persons, also known as the Trinity.

"Thanks for the history/theology lesson, Clay"—yawn, yawn—"but I thought this book was about how I can live in the promises of God in my life today?" It is. Those early church leaders understood something that many modern-day believers don't: a proper theological understanding of God leads to a powerful life with God in practice. To put it another way, if you don't have a proper understanding of the Holy Spirit you're going to struggle to experience the promises of God in your life. So what is it that we need to understand about the Holy Spirit and His power for our lives?

Who He Is—Part of the Triune Godhead

After Jesus' resurrection and shortly before He went back to heaven, He gave His followers a commission: "Go therefore and make disciples of all the nations, baptizing them in the name of the Father and the Son and the Holy Spirit" (Matthew 28:19). Notice the implied equality of the different persons of the Godhead in this passage. Baptism of those who came to faith was to be done in the name of all three persons of the Godhead.

In the apostle Paul's first letter to the church in Corinth, we again see an implied equality within the distinct persons of the Godhead: "There are different kinds of gifts, but the same Spirit distributes them. There are different kinds of service, but the same Lord. There are different kinds of working, but in all of them and in everyone it is the same God at work" (1 Corinthians 12:4–6 NIV).

As Paul closed out his second letter to the Corinthian church, he gave a closing salutation: "The grace of the Lord Jesus Christ, and the love of God, and the fellowship of the Holy Spirit, be with you all" (2 Corinthians 13:14). Again, all three persons of the Godhead are mentioned simultaneously and equally.

"How much more, then, will the blood of Christ, who through the eternal Spirit offered himself unblemished to God, cleanse our consciences from acts that lead to death, so that we may serve the living God!" (Hebrews 9:14 NIV). Notice in this last verse how all three persons of the Godhead are operating together to bring us into right relationship with God. And notice the eternal aspect of the Holy Spirit. Only God is truly eternal.

He Is Omnipresent—Nowhere That He Is Not

"Where can I go from your Spirit? Where can I flee from your presence? If I go up to the heavens, you are there; if I make my bed in the depths, you are there. If I rise on the wings of the dawn, if I settle on the far side of the sea, even there your hand will guide me, your right hand will hold me fast" (Psalm 139:7–10 NIV).

He Is Omnipotent—Nothing That He Cannot Do

"For the Spirit of God has made me, and the breath of the Almighty gives me life" (Job 33:4 NLT).

Jesus indicated that the miracles He performed were through the power of the Holy Spirit when He said, "But if I cast out demons by the Spirit of God, then the kingdom of God has come upon you" (Matthew 12:28).

He Is Omniscient—Nothing That He Does Not Know

"These are the things God has revealed to us by his Spirit. The Spirit searches all things, even the deep things of God. For who knows a person's thoughts except their own spirit within them? In the same way no one knows the thoughts of God except the Spirit of God" (1 Corinthians 2:10–11 NIV).

We could look at many more passages, but I think you get the point. What those early church leaders came to understand from God's Word, and what became a bedrock theological truth for the Orthodox Church, was the fact that the Holy Spirit is not an "it." The Holy Spirit is not God's helper. The Holy Spirit is certainly not some impersonal force. The Holy Spirit is God!

"Okay, the Holy Spirit is God. So what? I mean, no disrespect intended, but what difference does that make to my life? How does knowing that the Holy Spirit is God help me have more joy or worry less? How does knowing that the Holy Spirit is God help me live in the promises of God?" Come on; you know you were asking that question. And it's a great question. Are you ready for the answer? Why does it matter that we understand that the Holy Spirit is God?

What He Does—The Holy Spirit Lives in Us

I want you to think about that with me for a moment. Think about the implications of that truth for your life. If you have a personal relationship with Jesus Christ, God, the very God who spoke the world into existence, the God who flung the stars from His fingertips and holds them in place by His great power, that very same God dwells inside of you!

"And I will ask the Father, and he will give you another advocate to help you and be with you forever—the Spirit of truth. The world cannot accept him, because it neither sees him nor knows him. But you know him, for he lives with you and will be in you" (John 14:16–17 NIV).

"Don't you realize that all of you together are the temple of God and that the Spirit of God lives in you?" (1 Corinthians 3:16 NLT).

As they say in the tweet-o-sphere: "#Unbelievable! #Amazing! #Incredible!" Really, think about the implications of that truth for you. It means the Holy Spirit isn't something you have to "work up." The Holy Spirit doesn't have to "come down."

If you've given your life to Jesus Christ, God the Holy Spirit is in you right now, waiting for you to tap into His power for your life!

So exactly what is it that the Holy Spirit does for our lives? What does having the Holy Spirit residing in us mean for us?

He Helps Us

"I will ask the Father, and He will give you another Helper, that He may be with you forever" (John 14:16).

"But I tell you the truth, it is to your advantage that I go away; for if I do not go away, the Helper will not come to you; but if I go, I will send Him to you" (John 16:7).

"In the same way, the Spirit helps us in our weakness. We do not know what we ought to pray for, but the Spirit himself intercedes for us through wordless groans. And he who searches our hearts knows the mind of the Spirit, because the Spirit intercedes for God's people in accordance with the will of God" (Romans 8:26–27 NIV).

Of course, none of this makes the Holy Spirit subservient to us. Again, He's God, and God doesn't wait at our beck and call like some sort of personal concierge. What it does mean, though, is that He's there for us. He's not going to leave us in the middle of the messes of life. Because the Holy Spirit is God, He knows what we need before we do. So the worry that you feel over some situation, He wants to help you release it. The anger that you feel toward someone who has wronged you, He wants to help you forgive and be set free from the prison of bitterness. And because He's God, we know that He has the power to do all of that and more.

He Teaches Us

"But the Advocate, the Holy Spirit, whom the Father will send in my name, will teach you all things and will remind you of everything I have said to you" (John 14:26 NIV).

All of us have, at one time or another, said something like this: "I just wish I knew what to do." But when we operate in the power of the Holy Spirit, God promises that He will teach us exactly what we need to know for every situation.

Think about the stress and anxiety that will be released from your life if you know that the Holy Spirit will reveal to you what you need to do and when you need to do it. Think about the peace that will flood your soul because of your confidence in the knowledge that God will teach you what to do, how to do it, and when to do it.

He Gives Us Truth

"But when He, the Spirit of truth, comes, He will guide you into all the truth; for He will not speak on His own initiative, but whatever He hears, He will speak; and He will disclose to you what is to come" (John 16:13).

All of us have probably been misled before, perhaps by someone we thought we could trust, maybe by one of those so-called experts. Even our own feelings can mislead us. All of us have been deceived and have suffered as a result of the deception. God promises to give us truth. What a confidence booster to know that we have access to the one who will always give us the truth.

He Leads Us

In Acts chapter eight, the Spirit led Philip. "The Spirit told Philip, 'Go to that chariot and stay near it'" (Acts 8:29 NIV).

In Acts chapter ten, the Spirit led Peter. "While Peter was still thinking about the vision, the Spirit said to him, 'Simon, three men are looking for you. So get up and go downstairs. Do not hesitate to go with them, for I have sent them'" (Acts 10:19–20 NIV).

In Acts chapter sixteen, the Spirit led Paul and those with him.

> Paul and his companions traveled throughout the region of Phrygia and Galatia, having been kept by the Holy Spirit from preaching the word in the province of Asia. When they came to the border of Mysia, they tried to enter Bithynia, but the Spirit of Jesus would not

allow them to. So they passed by Mysia and went down to Troas. During the night Paul had a vision of a man of Macedonia standing and begging him, "Come over to Macedonia and help us." After Paul had seen the vision, we got ready at once to leave for Macedonia, concluding that God had called us to preach the gospel to them. —Acts 16:6–10 NIV

Notice in each instance that there was clear, specific leading by the Spirit of God. Did God love those early disciples more than He loves us today? Of course not. Is there any biblical reason to believe that God had specific plans for them, but not for us? Absolutely not.

Again, think about this for your own life: "Should I take this job offer?" "Is this the person I'm supposed to marry?" "Is college the right direction for me, and if so, which one?" I ask you again, is there any biblical reason you can think of that would indicate that God had specific plans for His disciples back then, but not for His disciples today?

At this point, you may be thinking, *Okay, I see where you're going with this, but the Holy Spirit was guiding Philip and Peter and Paul and the rest of them because they were on mission for Him. They were seeking to glorify Him and serve Him and make His name famous. I want to glorify God with my life, but how does this relate to the everyday decisions of my life? And is God's will always specific and clear?*

These are great observations—and even better questions! We're going to explore the relationship between God's guidance and life choices in the next chapter. For now, just be encouraged by the fact that the Spirit of God wants to lead us. "For those who are led by the Spirit of God are the children of God" (Romans 8:14 NIV). To turn that around and say it another way, if you're a child of God, you can expect to be led by the Spirit of God.

That may not be an exhaustive list of the roles the Holy Spirit performs in our lives, but I think it's enough to see that the Holy Spirit, who is God, dwells inside of followers of Jesus and not only wants them to live in the reality of God's promises, but also has the power to make it happen. The question then becomes, what do we have to do to tap into that power?

At least, I sure hope that's the question you're asking. It would be a shame to be this close to living in the promises of God and not desire to draw on the source of strength that will enable you to walk in them. It would be a tragedy to have the Spirit of God in your life and not experience His power for your life.

CHAPTER 5

HOW DO I BEGIN TO GET IT?

The world is a very religious place. In fact, in my opinion, one of the best evidences for the existence of God is the fact that the human race is incurably religious. Men and women the world over have differing ideas about who or what is God, but from the deepest jungle to the most remote snowcapped mountaintop, if you find people there, you will find them worshiping something.

Certainly there are those who claim that they don't believe in God and do not, therefore, have religious beliefs. That is, however, a conscious decision that they have made based on a personal choice—ironically enough, a personal choice that comes through God's granting to man free will. But the fact remains that no tribe or people group ever discovered has been totally void of the desire to worship and know God. Where does that inclination come from? Is there a religious gene? If mankind is simply another link in the evolutionary chain, at what point did it pick up the idea of God, and for what reason? And why is man the only creature that worships?

Some sociologists would suggest that man created the idea of God out of a deep-seated need within himself. Man's fear of the unknown, his inability to understand the mysteries of the universe gave birth to the idea of God as a sort of coping mechanism.

The purpose of this book is not to present an argument for the existence of God or to answer the skeptic's questions. Certainly there are many well-written books on the subject, and we Christians are encouraged to always be ready to give everyone an answer of why we believe what we believe (1 Peter 3:15).

The purpose of this book, however, is not to prove that God exists, but rather to help you discover how to live in the reality of God and His power. And by the way, even if you could prove that God existed, if you're not experiencing His power in your life on a daily basis, then what difference does it really make for you?

Nevertheless, the incurably religious nature of man does seem to indicate our understanding that we are not an island unto ourselves and that there is a God who has created us for a greater purpose. But there are a few things you have to understand to begin to get it.

You Don't Need a Religion—You Need a Relationship

Let's again look at Jesus' words in John 10: "My purpose is to give them a rich and satisfying life" (John 10:10 NLT). Jesus' purpose in coming was not to prove that God is. His purpose in coming was to provide what God offers. And what God offers is a relationship with Him, and that is very different from any man-made religion. It is, in fact, what separates true Christianity from every other religion in the world. Men and women seem to know instinctively that God exists, but what so many fail to see is that they exist for a relationship with God.

In Genesis chapter 5, "Enoch walked with God" (Genesis 5:22, 24). In Genesis chapter 6, "Noah walked with God" (Genesis 6:9). In Exodus 29, God stated that He would "dwell among His people" (Exodus 29:45). In Leviticus, God said He would "walk among you" (Leviticus 26:12). In Ezekiel, God stated that His "dwelling place" would be with His people (Ezekiel 37:27). Jesus said that God would "make His home with those who love Him" (John 14:23). He even called us His "friends" (John 15:15)!

Let me ask you a question. Does that sound like the words of a cold, distant, uncaring God, or one who desires for you to draw near to Him and to know Him personally and intimately?

Let me ask you another question. Does that describe what you have with God? Be honest now; would you say that you live in a vibrant, active, satisfying, personal relationship with the creator of the universe, one where you experience His joy and peace on a daily basis, where you receive His wisdom and power for your life, where you sense His presence and find purpose in discovering His will for you? Is that what you experience with God?

Or would you characterize what you have as more of a formal, ritualistic, dry, lifeless religion? Forget about Catholic, Baptist, Methodist, nondenominational, or whatever; do you live in the daily reality of God and His power? If not, your problem may be that you've got a religion about God, but not a relationship with God. Let me explain.

We've Have a Problem

On July 13, 1970, an oxygen tank ruptured, causing severe electrical damage to the Apollo 13 spacecraft and prompting commander Jim Lovell's now famous line, "Houston, we have a problem." What was intended to be the third landing on the moon in the Apollo space program turned into a monumental effort to save the lives of the three crew members on board the spacecraft.

Well, to have a relationship with God, you first have to realize that you have a problem. Can you imagine if the crew of Apollo 13 had simply ignored the obvious signs that there was a problem? It most certainly would have resulted in their deaths.

"Human race, we have a problem." And the problem is we are sinners. I'm sorry if that comes as a shock to you or insults you. And I know that our culture downplays the whole notion of sin, but the Bible makes it abundantly clear that all of us have violated Holy God's law.

"The fool says in his heart, 'There is no God.' They are corrupt, their deeds are vile; there is no one who does good. The LORD looks down from heaven on all mankind to see if there are any who understand, any who seek God. All have turned away, all have become corrupt; there is no one who does good, not even one" (Psalm 14:1–3; 53:1–3 NIV).

"What shall we conclude then? Do we have any advantage? Not at all! For we have already made the charge that Jews and Gentiles alike are all under the power of sin. As it is written: 'There is no one righteous, not even one; there is no one who understands; there is no one who seeks God' " (Romans 3:9–11 NIV).

"For all have sinned and fall short of the glory of God" (Romans 3:23 NIV).

People sometimes struggle with admitting that they have a sin problem. Think about it; do any of us really like to be told that we're wrong or that we've messed up? That would be a no. None of us enjoy being confronted with our sin. That's because our sin nature has a built-in defense mechanism; it's called pride. And our pride will do everything it can to keep us from acknowledging our own sinfulness.

To compound the problem, our culture is constantly promoting the idea that all of us are basically good. From the counselor's couch to the talk-show host, and sadly, even from many popular preachers and churches, the message is the same: "You're basically a good person." But as we've just seen, the Bible makes it crystal clear that none of us are good. The Bible makes it clear that we all have sinned.

Again, our pride attempts to mask the truth of our sinfulness by convincing us that while we may not be perfect, compared to some others we look pretty good. "Hey, compared to an ax murderer, I'm not such a bad guy." Okay, maybe that's an extreme, but the point is, when confronted with our own sinfulness, we look for someone else to blame or someone who's worse than we are.

However, someone else's life and actions aren't the standard by which we're measured. Our standard is God's righteous, holy perfection, and none of us measure up to that standard. We've all said, done, or thought something that God would not. That makes us sinners, and that's a problem. So if you want a relationship with God, you have to start by admitting that you have a problem, and the problem is you're a sinner.

There Is a Penalty

Sometimes people ask, "Why can't God just overlook our sin? You Christians are always saying that God is love. Well, if He loves us, why can't He just overlook our sin since none of us are perfect?"

The sentimental idea of a heavenly grandfather-type figure who makes allowances for our imperfections is a preferred view of God in a culture that prides itself on being nonjudgmental. There are, however, at least three issues with the idea that God should overlook our sin. For one thing, however much we'd like to do it:

We don't get to make the rules.

William Ernest Henley, in a poem titled "Invictus" (Latin for "unconquerable"), perfectly portrays the rebellious spirit of man when he proclaims, "I am the captain of my fate, / I am the master of my soul."[3] I'm sure there are plenty of people who would think that William Henley's declaration of defiance would make a great tattoo. But it doesn't make for great theology.

God is creator and owner of this whole thing. He is the one who decides what is and what is not. He's not running for reelection. He's doesn't make His decisions based on market research, public opinion, or popularity polls. He is God, and His word is final.

"You alone are the LORD. You have made the heavens, the heaven of heavens with all their host, the earth and all that is on it, the seas and all that is in them. You give life to all of them and the heavenly host bows down before You" (Nehemiah 9:6).

The second issue we run into when considering the idea that God should just overlook our sin is this:

It violates the very nature of God.

God will not be other than who He is, and He is holy and therefore cannot act in an unholy manner.

"You shall be holy, for I the LORD your God am holy" (Leviticus 19:2; 1 Peter 1:16).

"I am the LORD, your Holy One" (Isaiah 43:15).

"I am the Holy One" (Hosea 11:9 NCV).

"I am a holy God" (Amos 4:2 NCV).

Overlooking or ignoring sin would simply not be the act of a holy God. Because of His very nature sin must be dealt with. If a holy God has the capacity to determine what is sin, and the power to judge that sin, and does not, He cannot be considered holy. It would be an unholy act to allow un-holiness to exist and not deal with it in a holy manner.

One final reason why God can't simply overlook our sin:

Justice demands a penalty.

Suppose someone broke into your home, destroyed much of your property, and made off with thousands of dollars' worth of your valuables. Later the police catch the thief, and the trial date is set. The evidence is overwhelming. It's an open-and-shut case, and at the end of the trial, the thief is found guilty. But when he stands before the judge for sentencing, the judge says to the thief, "You know you shouldn't have done that. It was wrong of you to break into that house and steal someone else's stuff, but since I'm a nonjudgmental judge, I'm going to overlook the whole thing and act like it never happened. Court is adjourned."

Now tell the truth; what would you think of a judge who just overlooked the crimes of the guilty? You probably wouldn't think very much of that judge. You'd also demand that justice be done, including removing that judge from the bench!

So if you and I—sinful, imperfect people—can see the injustice in overlooking a crime, how can we possibly expect Holy God as judge to just overlook the crimes of the guilty? Because He is holy and just, His righteousness demands a penalty for our sin, and that penalty is death.

In Genesis chapter 2, after the creation of Adam, God said to him, "From any tree of the garden you may eat freely; but from the tree of the knowledge of good and evil you shall not eat, for in the day that you eat from it you shall surely die" (Genesis 2:16–17). You may be familiar with the rest of the story, but in Genesis chapter 3, Adam and Eve disobeyed God's command and ate the forbidden fruit. As a result, death entered God's creation that day. Adam and Eve began to die physically, but more importantly, they died spiritually. Their sin caused them to lose the relationship they had with God and to be separated from Him.

As much as we'd like to blame Adam and Eve for the troubles of this world, the truth is, all of us are to blame. As we've already established, we've all sinned. In essence, we've all eaten the forbidden fruit. We've all done things God would not want us to do, and therefore we're all guilty before the holy, righteous judge and under the same penalty as Adam and Eve.

"For the wages of sin is death" (Romans 6:23).

Science refers to it as the *second law of thermodynamics,* or the *law of entropy*. The Bible calls it the sin curse, but it's the same thing. Because of our sin, everything in the world is in a constant state of breakdown. Death, disease, deterioration, and destruction are constants in a world under the sin curse. "We know that all creation is still groaning and is in pain, like a woman about to give birth" (Romans 8:22 CEV).

The world spends billions of dollars on cosmetic surgeries and age-defying products. Many of us work out and try to eat right. The field of medicine is on a never-ending quest to increase both the quality and longevity of our lives, but despite man's best efforts, the death rate is still 100 percent. "And inasmuch as it is appointed for men to die once and after this comes judgment" (Hebrews 9:27).

"Thanks a lot, Mr. Sunshine. Would you like to kick my puppy now?" Wait, it gets worse! Not only are we in a physical state of dying, but spiritually speaking, we're already dead! The apostle Paul reminds us, "And you were dead in your trespasses and sins" (Ephesians 2:1).

There Is a Payment

What a hopeless, helpless mess we would be in if the story ended there. And nobody could blame God if it did.

How Do I Begin to Get It?

After all, we're the ones who rebelled against Him. As the prophet Isaiah reminds us, "All of us like sheep have gone astray, each of us has turned to his own way" (Isaiah 53:6). Fortunately for us, the story doesn't end there. God didn't leave us in our mess to suffer the consequences of our sin for all of eternity.

> But God, being rich in mercy, because of His great love with which He loved us, even when we were dead in our transgressions, made us alive together with Christ (by grace you have been saved), and raised us up with Him, and seated us with Him in the heavenly places in Christ Jesus, so that in the ages to come He might show the surpassing riches of His grace in kindness toward us in Christ Jesus. For by grace you have been saved through faith; and that not of yourselves, it is the gift of God; not as a result of works, so that no one may boast.
> —Ephesians 2:4–9

You could spend your lifetime searching the libraries of the world, reading both poetry and prose from every civilization throughout history, and you would never read words as beautiful, as important, and as powerful as those you just read from the apostle Paul's letter to the church at Ephesus.

To continue the judge analogy, after rightfully pronouncing us guilty of our sin and rightfully pronouncing the sentence on our sin (death), God, the holy righteous judge, did something absolutely astonishing. He stepped down from His position of authority and stepped into the position of the condemned. He laid down His life as payment for our sins.

"All of us like sheep have gone astray, each of us has turned to his own way; but the LORD has caused the iniquity of us all to fall on Him" (Isaiah 53:6).

"He made Him who knew no sin to be sin on our behalf, so that we might become the righteousness of God in Him" (2 Corinthians 5:21).

There Is a Promise

It defies all reason or logic. Why would God do that for us? He certainly didn't have to. Jesus said, "No one has taken it away from Me [His life], but I lay it down on My own initiative" (John 10:18).

Why would God make payment for the very ones who had rebelled against Him? Certainly not to meet any need that He had. God wasn't incomplete. God wasn't lonely. God doesn't need anything. God isn't any less God with or without us. So why would the one who is holy, righteous, and perfect lay down His life for ones who are unholy, unrighteous, and imperfect? Are you ready for this?

God simply chose to love us and have a relationship with us, and by doing so, He condemned Himself to suffer and die as the perfect, sinless, substitutionary sacrifice for our sins. He made it possible for broken, sinful people to be forgiven, made whole, and adopted into His family!

"Therefore there is now no condemnation for those who are in Christ Jesus. For the law of the Spirit of life in Christ Jesus has set you free from the law of sin and of death" (Romans 8:1–2).

"That if you confess with your mouth Jesus as Lord, and believe in your heart that God raised Him from the dead, you will be saved; for with the heart a person believes, resulting in righteousness, and with the mouth he confesses, resulting in salvation" (Romans 10:9–10).

What a promise! It doesn't matter who you are or what you've done. It doesn't matter your age or skin color or educational level or social status. It doesn't matter how good you think you've been or how bad. We've all sinned against God. The great news is this:

> But God demonstrates His own love toward us, in that while we were yet sinners, Christ died for us. —Romans 5:8

> For God so loved the world, that He gave His only begotten Son, that whoever believes in Him shall not perish, but have eternal life. For God did not send the Son into the world to judge the world, but that the world might be saved through Him. —John 3:16–17

As difficult as it may be to get our minds around it, the greatest truth you and I will ever hear is that God would rather die than live without us.

And that's exactly what He did. He made the way so that you and I could be forgiven and adopted into the family of God and have a personal relationship with Him. The former slave ship captain John Newton called it "amazing grace." Pastor and author Francis Chan calls it "crazy love." You can call it yours, if you will let go of religion and ritual and embrace a relationship with God based on His gift of eternal life.

We've Got a Purpose

This leads to one more idea in the first step toward being in the right position to receive God's power: we've got a purpose. One of the consequences for our culture's teaching that we're just a cosmic accident, just another rung on the evolutionary ladder, is that it leads to the logical conclusion that there is no real meaning to life. Without God, there is no purpose to our lives.

When someone doesn't have a relationship with God, they seek satisfaction in the things of the world to give purpose to their life. It's a life filled with thrill seeking or possession accumulation or chemical stimulation. It's a life that is always searching, but never satisfied. It is a life that tries to fill the void with fun and fantasy. It's a life destined to fail because it will never deliver what our souls are ultimately longing for—a relationship with God.

When I was in college, we had a guest speaker who was from Russia. He was a brilliant man with multiple PHDs. He had been high up in the Russian government prior to the fall of communism and before he became a follower of Jesus. For seventy years, communism taught the people that there was no God. Politically, socially, economically and philosophically, communism, they were told, was all that they needed. With the collapse of communism, a collective void was left in the hearts of the Russian people.

As our guest spoke that day, he shared with us how alcoholism had become so prevalent in Russia. He spoke of the emptiness of the people's lives. He spoke of the hopelessness and despair that the people lived with. He said you could see it in their eyes. I'll never forget these next words he spoke. He pointed his finger at his chest and with a thick Eastern European accent he said:

"*Everyone have in them the God-spot.*"

I still remember feeling absolutely stunned by his words. I'd never thought about it in those terms, but he was exactly right. Everybody does have the "God-spot." We, as the human race, try to fill it with anything and everything when it really can be filled only by one thing: a relationship with God. It's that relationship that brings meaning and purpose into our lives. It's that relationship that is fulfilling. It's satisfying. In a word, it's living!

"For we are His workmanship, created in Christ Jesus for good works, which God prepared beforehand so that we would walk in them" (Ephesians 2:10).

The God-spot can't be filled by a religion *about* God. It can be filled only by a relationship *with* God. The reason: Religion is a ceremony, and a relationship is a celebration. Religion is ritual, and a relationship is real. Religion is performance, and a relationship is personal.

Maybe the most beautiful picture of this in the entire Bible is found in Jesus' parable about the prodigal son (Luke 15). The story is about a father with two sons. One of his sons demanded his inheritance even while his father was still alive because he didn't want to wait until his father passed away to use his father's money the way the son chose.

Can you imagine going to your mom and dad and saying, "Hey, listen. I know you're going to kick it someday anyway, so why don't you just go ahead and give me my inheritance so I can go out and party like a rock star now and not have to wait for you to die?" I don't know about you, but if I had said that to my dad, he would have "kicked it," all right. He would have kicked my tail up one side of the street and down the other!

Anyway, back to Jesus' story. The father granted his son's request and gave him his inheritance. The prodigal son went off and did exactly what you knew he was going to do: he wasted every bit of his inheritance on what he thought would make him happy, on what he thought would fill the God-spot.

Eventually the money ran out, the wine ran out, and of course when that happened, his friends ran out. And there he sat, literally in the middle of a pig pen—no money, no food, no friends, nothing. As Jesus put it, the young man finally "came to his senses" (Luke 15:17) and realized, like Dorothy in *The Wizard of Oz*, "there's no place like home."[4]

Unlike Dorothy, though, there were no ruby-red slippers that he could just slip into and click three times to take him back to his father's house—not that he had any hope of being accepted back by his father as a son. The prodigal knew he had blown that one, but he thought if he could just get a job working for his father, he'd at least be able to eat. Now here's where the story gets really good. I'll let Jesus tell it:

> So he got up and came to his father. But while he was still a long way off, his father saw him and felt compassion for him, and ran and embraced him and kissed him. And the son said to him, "Father, I have sinned against heaven and in your sight; I am no longer worthy to be called your son." But the father said to his slaves, "Quickly bring out the best robe and put it on him, and put a ring on his hand and sandals on his feet; and bring the fattened calf, kill it, and let us eat and celebrate; for this son of mine was dead and has come to life again; he was lost and has been found." And they began to celebrate.
> —Luke 15:20–24

I want to ask you what I asked you earlier: does that sound like a religion, or does that sound like a relationship? The father who had been disrespected, dishonored, and was no doubt disappointed had every right to tell his son to buzz off. He had every right to say, "Get off my land!" No one would have blamed him if he had said, "You had your chance and you blew it! You are no longer my son." But the father didn't do that, did he? In fact, not only did he allow his wayward son to come back home, but the father actually ran out to meet him! And did you catch this line: "But while he was still a long way off, his father saw him"?

Talk about crazy love! The father was waiting for his son to come home the whole time! I can imagine, as the father made his way into the fields day after day, his eyes scanned the horizon in search of his prodigal son. Every time he stood up to stretch his sore, bent-over back, he stole a glance to see if this might be the day. When he wiped the sweat from his face, when he reached the end of a row with his plow, when he gathered the herds, each and every time his eyes turned to the distance and strained to see his long-lost son.

And when that day finally arrived, rather than stand there with his arms crossed and wait for his sinful son to come crawling back to him, like most of us probably would have demanded, the father hiked up his robe and took off running as fast as he could to meet his wayward son. As the King James Version puts it, when the father got to his prodigal son, he "fell on his neck, and kissed him" (Luke 15:20). What a powerful expression of compassion and love! What a picture of relationship!

Some people might say that wasn't very dignified of the father. They may be right, but if you're a father, you probably get it. The father didn't give his son what he deserved. He gave his son what he needed. He gave his son grace.

It's not too hard to figure out that in Jesus' story, the father represents God, and the prodigal, well, that's you and me. We've gone our own way and tried to find happiness and fill the spot with anything and everything the world has to offer. We're like the hamster in the cage on the little wheel. We're in a big hurry to get to our destination, but we never really arrive. We're really just spinning our wheels.

As a native of Florida, I'm familiar with greyhound dog racing. Dogs come out of a starting gate and chase a mechanical rabbit or lure around a track. People bet on which dog they think will finish the course the fastest.

The irony is that the dogs have been trained to catch something that they're not actually allowed to catch. The speed of the lure is monitored and adjusted as needed to ensure that no matter how hard a dog may work, no matter how fast a dog may run, he will never catch what he so desperately wants. As a matter of fact, if the dog should ever happen to catch the lure as a result of mechanical failure, it's considered a "no race." It's like the race was never run. How beat up is that? Even if the dog achieves his goal, it doesn't count!

Most people spend their lives chasing the elusive lure. We are trained by our culture to believe that if we can catch it, then we'll be satisfied. Sadly, though, our lure manages to always stay just ahead of us.

You and I were created for a greater purpose than chasing the lures of this world. You and I were created to live in the reality of a loving God. We have purpose. Our lives have meaning. We're not cosmic accidents. God invites us to know Him and to experience the fullness of a life built on the promises and power of God. But try as you might, you'll never find any of it in a religion. You need a relationship. And you need to ask yourself if you understand the difference and which one you possess.

So the first step to being in the right position to tap into the power of God and thereby live in the promises of God is to know that you don't need a religion—you need a relationship. The second step may surprise you.

Chapter 6

Am I in Position for It?

I'm a bit of a golfer. I'm not a great golfer, but I am a student of the game. One of the things that has always fascinated me about golf is how much power the professionals generate in their swing with what appears to be so little effort. While their swings look effortless compared to mine, they generate far more clubhead speed, which translates into the ball going farther, much farther, than I can hit it.

They make it look so easy. They make it look like they don't even have to work at it. I hate them! Not really. Actually, I envy them. I would like to swing easier and hit it farther—any golfer would. So how do they do it?

The answer is position. A golf swing is made up of many different components: spine angle, arms, hands, shoulders, head, lower body, clubface, shaft angle, swing plane, and more. All of these components must come together in perfect symmetry to be able to generate maximum power. Everything has to be in the right position to get the power.

By the way, the pros make it look effortless, but it's not. It may look like they don't even have to work at it, but they do. As a matter of fact, that's probably the number one difference between a professional golfer and a weekend hacker. Professionals put in tens of thousands of hours on the range. They hit probably hundreds of thousands of golf balls, all in an effort to create a swing that brings everything together in perfect position to generate the greatest amount of power possible.

Think about it. Haven't you met those people who just seem to make the Christian life look easy? Granted, they are rare, but aren't there Christians that you've watched and thought, *How do they do it? It doesn't even seem like they have to work at it.* But is the spiritual life really easier for those Christians? Or do they just approach it differently? What do they do to have what looks like effortless spiritual power in their lives?

The answer: They understand that in order to be spiritually empowered in life, they have to be in the right position for maximum power. And just like the golfers who have effortless-looking swings, Christians living in the reality of the power of God may make it look easy, but I assure you, it is not.

Followers of Jesus who get it have taken the steps necessary to be in position to experience God's power. In the last chapter, we looked at what we need to experience God's power: having a relationship with God, not a religion about God. In this chapter, we're going to spend time looking at how to be in the right position in order to tap into the power of God and thereby live in the promises of God—in other words, being in position to get it. Here's what you need to know:

You Don't Need to Be Happy—You Need to Be Holy

"Okay, that does it. You're telling me that God doesn't want me to be happy?" Well, sort of. What I'm saying is that most people spend their lives trying to be happy. Most people assume that doing what pleases them is what will make them happy. God says that's a formula for disaster and a wasted life.

Pleasing God instead of yourself might sound like you get the short end of the stick. But here's the really cool part: when you choose to please God with your life, that's when you actually discover what it really means to be happy! That's when you understand that your idea of happiness or the world's idea of happiness is really nothing more than a cheap imitation of what God really wants you to experience.

Start a discussion on what is the greatest movie of all time, and opinions are as numerous as Google searches for the Kardashian sisters. But as far as I'm concerned, one word says it all—*Casablanca*. This 1942 film starring Humphrey Bogart and Ingrid Bergman is for me a masterpiece of cinematic art. (Listen to me; I sound like Roger Ebert.)

Yes, it's in black and white (which actually makes it better, by the way), and no, it's not the greatest special effects you'll ever see (if you look closely, you can actually see the guide wire that the model airplane is attached to as it takes off), but the characters, acting, music, and dialogue have all become iconic.

In the storyline, which takes place in early World War II, the two main characters, Rick and Ilsa, are forced to choose between doing what they think will make them happy and what is right. They are in love, and they want to be together. But they find out that Ilsa's husband, who they thought had been killed by the Germans, is in fact alive.

I don't want to give away too much of the plot, in case you haven't seen it, and I'm not necessarily extolling the moral virtues of Rick and Ilsa, but the story points to the biblical truth that being happy is not the most important thing in life. I know that statement flies in the face of contemporary wisdom and public opinion, but as I've already stated, God's not really concerned about public opinion.

Earlier we established that God is a holy God. It means He is set apart, unlike any other. We also established the fact that God calls us to be holy. Obviously, we aren't holy in the exact same sense that God is holy. God is sinless. God is perfection. You and I are neither of those things, but as His adopted children with His Spirit abiding in us, we are called to set ourselves apart from a world that chooses its will over God's.

> Do not be bound together with unbelievers; for what partnership have righteousness and lawlessness, or what fellowship has light with darkness? Or what harmony has Christ with Belial, or what has a believer in common with an unbeliever? Or what agreement has the temple of God with idols? For we are the temple of the living God; just as God said, "I will dwell in them and walk among them; and I will be their God, and they shall be My people. Therefore, come out from their midst and be separate," says the Lord. "And do not touch what is unclean; and I will welcome you." —2 Corinthians 6:14–17

Did you hear in Paul's words the relationship aspect that we looked at earlier? Look at those relational phrases like "dwell in them," "walk among them," "I will be their God, and they shall be My people." Again we see that God's desire is for us to have something with Him that is personal, but notice the conditional clause: "and do not touch what is unclean; and I will welcome you."

We're not talking about sinless perfection here. The Bible makes it very clear that all of us sin. That's why Jesus came in the first place: to pay a debt that we ourselves could never pay. But when we enter into that relationship with God, He moves us away from our old way of life and moves us toward a life of holiness.

One time I had a conversation with my then four-year-old grandson Wyatt about not hitting his then two-year-old brother Dakota. The conversation went something like this:

"Wyatt, did you hit Dakota?"
"Yes."
"Did I tell you not to hit your brother?"
"Yes."
"Then why did you hit your brother?"
And without any hesitation at all and seemingly without any remorse, Wyatt said: "Because I wanted to, Poppie."

To Wyatt (and any other child), choosing what made him happy over what was right was the most natural thing in the world. And that's true. Our sin nature is always leading us to please ourselves.

Sadly, though, that's the same type of response I've gotten from men and women that I've confronted (as their pastor) over choices they've made that were clearly contrary to God's will and God's Word—men and women who claimed that Jesus was their Lord and Savior, but who had clearly chosen a path of their own making and not God's. I can still hear it: "Well, I just think God wants me to be happy." Oh, really? Would you like to show me anywhere in God's Word where God wanted someone to be happy at the expense of being holy?

Keep in mind that being holy means to be set apart, to choose differently from what the world would choose. The world will always choose self, and God calls us to deny self. The world will say, "It makes me feel good. I deserve to be happy." God says, "That's a life that will leave you shallow, empty, and unfulfilled."

Now, if I've left you with the impression that choosing holiness means that we have to live our lives wearing drab brown-hooded robes and spend our days locked away from the world inside some dark monastery, reciting ancient Gregorian chants in unison, then I apologize. Nothing could be further from the truth.

Of course, that's the way the world looks at it, doesn't it? God is the giant cosmic killjoy who doesn't want anybody to have fun. That view of what it means to follow Christ is summed up perfectly in a popular Billy Joel song titled "Only the Good Die Young":

> And they say there's a heaven for those who will wait.
>
> Some say it's better, but I say it ain't.
>
> I'd rather laugh with the sinners than cry with the saints.
>
> The sinners have much more fun.
>
> You know that only the good die young.[4]

Billy Joel may be a brilliant songwriter, but he's a lousy theologian, because first, the "good" aren't the only ones that die young. None of us are promised tomorrow, and death eventually comes to everyone, with judgment to follow (Hebrews 9:27).

Second, sinners don't have "much more fun." And shame on us Christians if we've helped to perpetuate that misconception by acting as if following Jesus and choosing holiness is some kind of sentence to be endured rather than a life of freedom to be enjoyed!

Years ago, a pastor of mine, Dick Whipple, used to say, "Too many Christians act like they were baptized in vinegar." The famous preacher Vance Havner used to say, "Too many church services start at eleven o'clock sharp and end at twelve o'clock dull."

What's wrong with us? Shouldn't followers of Jesus have the most fun in life? Shouldn't we display peace, joy, and contentment in our lives in such abundance that the world wants to know about the source of our unfathomable happiness? Shouldn't the world actually envy us because of what they see in our lives?

Could it be that too many Christians still don't get it? Experiencing the promises of God that make our lives fulfilling and rewarding comes only when we live in the reality of His power. His power comes only when we're in the right position to receive it, and being in the right position requires choosing God's holiness over what the world thinks is happiness.

Being in position to receive God's power and therefore live in the reality of His promises requires meeting the prerequisite of having a relationship, not a religion, as discussed in chapter 5. And as we've seen in this chapter, being in position to receive His power requires holiness, not happiness. There's one more truth to consider if you're going to be in the right position to receive God's power:

You Don't Need to Serve—You Need to Surrender

Now you really do think I've flipped a brick, don't you—a pastor who doesn't want people to serve? Again, that's not exactly what I mean. Service to both the body and to the world around us is vitally important and clearly a biblical mandate. But too many Christians see their service to God as evidence that they are in the will of God, when in fact that may not be the case. And if you're not in the will of God, you're not in position to receive and experience His power.

Before my call to be a pastor, I worked for the United States Postal Service for several years. At one time, I worked with an older gentleman named Robert. He was a good Christian guy. He was active in his church. He actively served both his church and community. One day Robert began to tell me about how as a young man he had sensed God's call on his life to be a missionary overseas. Whatever all the reasons were, Robert didn't answer that call. He got married, had children, and settled into a good life in his hometown. As I said, he was active in church and served faithfully.

Robert told me that story several times while we worked together, and he never once told it to me without tears filling his eyes and without choking back emotional regret. Robert was a good man. His service to his church and community was needed, but our service is never a substitute for our surrender.

Maybe this is a good time to just stop and ask, are you surrendered to God? "Well, I serve in the nursery twice a month." "I serve as a greeter." "I attend a Bible study every week." "I tithe, for goodness' sake!" All of those things are fine and good and important, but it doesn't answer the question. Are you surrendered to God?

Don't misunderstand me; things like service and stewardship and study are part of a surrendered life. But God requires absolute and complete surrender of every aspect of our lives to Him, and anything less than that is less than God wants for us.

And notice that I said, "wants *for* us," not "wants *from* us." This has never been about what we can do for God to somehow gain His approval. This is about what God wants us to have. He wants us to have abundant life. He wants us to live in the reality of His power. He wants us to experience a life built on the promises of God, and the Bible makes it abundantly clear that can occur only when there is unconditional surrender.

At the church I pastor in Raleigh, North Carolina, Cross Culture Church, we have something we call our passion statement: "Taking the cross to our culture, taking our culture to the cross." We never want to forget that we are called to take the message of Jesus to the world, a message that centers on the cross of Christ, where His sacrifice purchased salvation for all who would come to Him. As we are faithful to deliver that message and as the Holy Spirit draws people to Him, they become fully devoted followers of Jesus with an understanding that they are called, in a sense, to the cross. We are called to die to self and to live for Christ—in a word, *surrender*. I say again, anything less than that is less than God wants for us.

Our theme verse at Cross Culture Church is Luke 9:23, which says, "And He was saying to them all, 'If anyone wishes to come after Me, he must deny himself, and take up his cross daily and follow Me' " (Luke 9:23).

Every once in a while, you'll hear someone say something like, "That's just my cross to bear," referring to some trial or circumstance or situation they're going through that they have to endure. But that's not really what Jesus was getting at in this verse. Two thousand years ago, the cross was a standard form of execution. The Assyrians, the Persians, the Carthaginians, the Greeks, and then the Romans practiced crucifixion for hundreds of years. The people of Jesus' day knew all too well that the cross was an instrument of death, so they also would have understood Jesus' intended meaning: that if you want to be His disciple, you have to choose every day to die to yourself and be completely surrendered to Him.

In the euphoria of post–World War II, America experienced what can only be described as a boom time. The economy boomed, businesses boomed, towns and cities boomed, families boomed (hence the phrase *baby-boomer generation*), and churches boomed as well.

Long before Kevin Costner's character Ray Kinsella (*Field of Dreams*) heard a voice in his cornfield whisper, "If you build it, he will come," church leaders and denominational heads were shouting, "If you build it, they will come!" Churches sprang up everywhere, and practically before the paint dried on the steeple, in they came. Pews were filling up, Sunday school classes were filling up, and church rolls were filling up.
But in the rush to get people in the front door, it seems that something got pushed out the back; namely, a biblical understanding of what it really means to be a fully devoted follower of Jesus. The call to come to Christ has always included a call to complete, total, and unconditional surrender. Certainly the early church understood this truth.

Steven Curtis Chapman's song "For the Sake of the Call" expresses it well:

> Nobody stood and applauded them
>
> So they knew from the start this road would not lead to fame
>
> All they really knew for sure was Jesus had called to them
>
> He said, "Come follow me" and they came
>
> With reckless abandon they came
>
> Empty nets lying there at the water's edge
>
> Told a story that few could believe or none could explain

> How some crazy fishermen agreed to go where Jesus led
>
> With no thought for what they would gain
>
> For Jesus had called them by name and they answered
>
> We will abandon it all for the sake of the call
>
> No other reason at all but the sake of the call
>
> Wholly devoted to live and to die for the sake of the call.[5]

Unfortunately, in the second half of the twentieth century and into the twenty-first, many professing followers of Jesus in America began to think of their faith as "part" of their lives. There was work, there was family, there were Little League games and Girl Scout meetings and a hundred other activities that prosperity brings with it, and somewhere in the midst of their increasingly hectic lifestyles, there was their faith. The problem is, Jesus didn't die so that He could be a part of your life. He died so that you could have real life in Him! And that requires surrender to Him.

Don't get me wrong; the church should want to grow. We should do all we can to bring people in the front door. We should reach out to those around us who don't have a relationship with Jesus Christ. I would certainly rather preach to people than to empty seats. But helping people understand what it means to find Jesus means helping them understand what it means to lose themselves in Jesus. Jesus said as much when He proclaimed: "And he who does not take his cross and follow after Me is not worthy of Me. He who has found his life will lose it, and he who has lost his life for My sake will find it" (Matthew 10:38–39).

So at the risk of thoroughly ticking you off, I ask again, are you surrendered to God, or are you just serving God? The church I pastor, like most churches, has plenty of needs for people to serve, but the greater need is for surrender. If a person surrenders his or her life to Jesus Christ, truly surrenders, you won't have to worry about whether he or she is going to serve.

Like I said at the beginning of this chapter, the pro golfer who produces all of that power makes it look easy, but it's not. He or she has learned how to get everything in the right position to generate maximum power. And the follower of Jesus who makes it look easy knows that it's not. Followers of Jesus understand the prerequisite of having a relationship with God instead of a religion about God. They've chosen God's holiness over the world's happiness. And they've learned that service is not the same thing as surrender.

When you meet the prerequisite and are in position to live and operate in God's power, His promises begin to manifest themselves in your life. His peace, His love, His joy begin to replace your fear, your stress, your anxiety, your anger. God begins to produce the life His Word promised you could have. So if that sounds like something you'd be interested in, keep going.

Chapter 7
Am I Prepared for It?

Have you seen the television show *Doomsday Preppers*? It's a show about people who are convinced that it's only a matter of time before our world faces a cataclysmic disaster from either a financial collapse, a nuclear disaster, a giant meteor collision, an electromagnetic-pulse (EMP) detonation, or some other natural or man-made disaster that is going to change life as we know it forever.

Assuming that Jack Bauer won't be around to save us (shout-out to fans of *24*), these people are gearing up for those future events by preparing for life the day after it all goes down. Families are building bunkers under their basements. They are storing up food to last for years. They've prepared bug-out bags so that they're ready to go at a moment's notice. They've got escape routes all mapped out to take them to some remote area where they can live off the grid—all of this and more in preparation for the hard life that they believe could possibly be coming.

Well, not to make light of the end-of-the-world predictors, but as we discussed earlier, life is already hard! Maybe it's not as physically hard as it's going to be if any of those doomsday scenarios comes true, but physically, emotionally, and spiritually, we all face challenges.

So maybe we need to take a page from the preppers' playbook? But what's important to understand, and what this chapter is about, is that God is the one who's going to do the prepping in our lives, not us. Let me explain what I mean.

Among other things, up to this point we've learned that to live in the promises of God, we need to have His power. Without God's power in our lives, we're really like the ninety-pound weakling on the beach, and our circumstances and trials are the bully kicking sand in our face. Simply put, we can't have the promises of God if we don't have the power of God. And, in order to have that power, we have to be in a relationship with God. Additionally, as we discovered in the last chapter, in order to have His power working in us, we have to be in the right position.

So let's say we've taken it that far. We've chosen relationship over religion. We've chosen holiness over worldly happiness, and we've chosen surrender over simply serving. Now what? How do we begin to feel His peace and strength and live in the promises of God?

Okay, this is going to sound weird, but if you want to live in the promises of God, this is what you need to know: cows like country music. Perhaps I should elaborate. When you grow up on a dairy farm you learn in a hurry that there are a lot of things that have to be done on a on a daily basis (at this point, my older brothers are wondering how I could possibly know that since they claim I was always off playing when they were working), but the bottom line, the end goal for the dairy farmer, is production. You want—correction, you need—your cows to produce. A dairy farmer won't stay in business very long if his cows aren't producing milk. Chick-fil-A has made a lot of money with cows producing billboards extolling the virtue of eating more chicken, but a dairy farmer knows that he won't make a dime unless his cows produce milk.

You might be tempted to say, "What's the big deal? You feed them some hay and milk comes out." Not so fast, my bovine-challenged friend. It's a little more complicated than that. A farmer knows that in order for his cows to be good milk producers, they need a routine—everything from the type of feed they eat, to the time of day they're milked, and yes, even to the music that's playing in the barn. It's all a part of a cow's routine. If the cows don't have a routine or their routine gets thrown off, even changing the radio station from what they're used to (for our cows, it was country), it will affect the amount and quality of the milk they produce. A routine is critical to good production.

Well, for there to be spiritual production in our lives we need what cows need. If you want to live in the promises of God on a daily basis, you need a routine. We need a spiritual routine. Now I didn't say that it should *be* routine, as in boring or dull—far from it. Our spiritual journey should, and can be, exciting, fresh, and challenging. Like our four-legged friends down on the farm, however, unless we have a routine, the production of the promises of God in your life and mine will suffer. Here's why.

We already established back in chapter 2 that we have three enemies working against us: the devil who deceives, the world that distracts, and our own flesh that desires. They're always trying to pull us away from the things of God. They're always trying to instill fear, steal peace, create anxiety, cause anger, and get us to focus on our circumstances. They're trying to create in us the polar opposite of what God wants us to have. They are, in effect, the anti-promises.

We've also looked at the fact that we don't have what it takes to overcome those three enemies of our spiritual walk and be able to experience the promises of God in our lives on a daily basis. In ourselves, in our own strength, we'll lose.

Spiritually speaking, on our own, we've brought a knife to a gunfight, and it doesn't take a lot of imagination to see how that's going to come out. To borrow a line from Clint Eastwood in *The Outlaw Josey Wales*, "Dyin' ain't much of a livin', boy."[6]

That's where most people are in their lives. They're alive, but not really. They're like spiritual zombies, walking around, going through the motions of daily life, but missing the life God intended for them because they haven't tapped into the power that God makes available to them, the power that makes real life possible. They just don't get it.

So again, being in position to receive the power is critical. I know we've been through all that already, but I'm not sure that it can be overstated. You've got to make sure you have a relationship with Jesus Christ and not just a religion. Also, you've got to make a choice for holiness instead of the world's counterfeit idea of happiness. And you've got to make a point to surrender, not just serve. If you don't get those three imperatives right, then none of the rest of this will make a difference.

Now here's the reason a spiritual routine becomes so important to seeing the promises of God produced in your life, because as Ron Lee Davis puts it in his commentary on Romans chapter 12:

> *"That's the problem with a living sacrifice:*
> *it keeps crawling off the altar."*[7]

In other words, even though we may genuinely have a personal relationship with Jesus Christ, that relationship, if we let it, can grow cold or distant. It's not that God moves or changes, but we allow things to come between God and us that interfere with our relationship with God.

Making a choice for holiness instead of worldly happiness is wonderful, but it's a choice that has to be made again and again because there will always be the temptation to please self instead of choosing holiness. There will always be temptations that lure us toward rebellion against God.

Making a decision to surrender all of our life instead of just giving God a portion in service is the right decision to make, but it's not a one-and-done deal. Oh, if only it were that easy! But the devil is still trying to deceive, the world is still trying to distract, and our flesh still desires what it desires. It's one thing to sing the old hymn "I Surrender All"; it's another thing to actually live a surrendered life every day.

The apostle Paul says in Romans 12:1, "Therefore I urge you, brethren, by the mercies of God, to present your bodies a living and holy sacrifice, acceptable to God, which is your spiritual service of worship" (Romans 12:1).

Notice he says, "brethren" (or "brothers"), so he's talking to people who have already made the decision to follow Jesus. But he urges us to daily, continually present our bodies. In other words, we have to consciously, continually choose to honor God with our lives. We have to intentionally lay down our lives and wills to be in position for God to produce His power in our lives.

Power Pattern

That's why we need a spiritual routine or, what I'll call a *power pattern*. It's a pattern you and I can follow to tap into God's power. My preaching professor in seminary, Dr. Wayne McDill, used to tell us that we were doing people a disservice when we preached if we told them what was wrong but didn't give them the solution.

In the last two chapters we looked at the three steps—relationship not religion, holiness not happiness, surrender not serve—for being in position to receive God's power. Those steps are intended to move you in the right direction to accomplish the objective of living in the promises of

God. But to continue to see the promises of God produced in your life on a daily basis I offer you this power pattern to follow. First:

Prepare

I was never a Boy Scout, but I know their motto: "Be prepared." Whether you're planning a wedding, planning a trip, planning on opening a business, or almost anything else you can think of, preparation is vital.

What about those of you who grow gardens? Personally, I find the produce section at the grocery store much easier, but for those who like to play in the dirt, do you just go outside as growing season arrives and throw a few seeds on the ground? Probably not. There is normally a good bit of prep work that has to be done before the seeds go into the ground. I know there can be other factors, but when it comes to growing produce, usually the more you prepare, the more that is produced. Guess what? The same thing is true when we talk about the promises of God being produced in our lives. There has to be preparation.

Now in this planting analogy, it's important to remember that it's not you or me doing the producing—it's God. You and I are, well, we're the dirt—which is not such a stretch when you think about the fact that the first man, Adam, was formed from "the dust from the ground" (Genesis 2:7). But unlike the dirt, you and I have free will, and with it we must make some choices.

I know that God is sovereign. I know that His ultimate purposes and plans for His creation will be fulfilled, but I also know that the Bible clearly teaches that man has a free will. We can find plenty of places in the Bible where God desired one thing for the people, but they chose something else. For instance, starting all the way back in the Garden of Eden, God said, "Do not eat from the tree of the knowledge of good and evil" (Genesis 2:17). But Adam and Eve ate of that fruit. God wanted one thing for them, but Adam and Eve chose another (see Genesis 3).

God led the people of Israel to the edge of the Promised Land, but they rebelled against God and would not enter in because they were scared of the people living in the land. God wanted one thing for the people, but they chose another (see Numbers 14). Later on, God told the people of Israel they didn't need an earthly king; He would be their king. But the Israelites wanted to be like the other nations around them and have an earthly king. God wanted one thing for the people, but they chose another (see 1 Samuel 8 and 10).

In the New Testament, Jesus' heart broke as He reflected on the choices His people had made, when He said, "Jerusalem, Jerusalem, who kills the prophets and stones those who are sent to her! How often I wanted to gather your children together, the way a hen gathers her chicks under her wings, and you were unwilling" (Matthew 23:37). Notice, it wasn't that they *could* not choose to follow God, but that they *would* not. Once again, God wanted one thing for the people, but they chose another.

Now in each case, the sovereignty of God was always a step ahead of the rebellion of men so that God's ultimate plans and purposes were always fulfilled. And exactly how the sovereignty of God and the free will of man work together is something probably best left lost in the mystery of the Godhead. But quite honestly, a fatalistic approach to life that says, "Well, if it's God's will, it will work out" is a flawed understanding of our relationship to God, and it attempts to allow men and women to shirk their responsibility before God. The bottom line is, you and I have been asked to make some choices.

God tells us that He will give us peace. He will give us contentment. He will take our fear away. He will give us joy. He will give us purpose. He will give us all of those promises that we looked at earlier that He says we can have and that He wants us to have, if we will take hold of them. The question then becomes, do you want to take hold of the promises of God? (Hopefully, you've settled that one!) And, are you willing to do what you have to do to live in the reality of the promises of God? If so, there has to be some prep work.

So specifically, what do we need to do in the way of preparation, or more exactly, what do we need to allow God to do to us to prepare us for production? Let's continue the planting analogy.

Broken Up

As I understand it, one of the first things that has to be done in preparation in order to produce results in farming is to break up the soil. Especially after a cold, hard winter, the ground can become compacted and hard. The soil won't allow air in and is unreceptive to the seeds. It makes it difficult for anything of value to grow.

In preparation for the power of God to produce the promises of God, you and I have to allow the Holy Spirit to break up the hardness. We may not even be aware that our lives have become hard and unproductive. Circumstances, events, trials, and even just plain busyness can harden our spirits toward the things of God. We have to ask Him to make us sensitive to areas where we may have become hard and then ask the Spirit of God to break up those hard spots in our hearts and make our lives receptive to His work. Quite honestly, this can be a difficult time as the Holy Spirit reveals to us the ways that we have hardened ourselves to His working in our lives. It is a deeply personal and often painful experience, but it's absolutely essential if we're going to see the His promises produced in our lives.

Cleaned Up

After the soil has been turned over and broken up, it has to be cleaned up. In other words, it has to be weeded to remove whatever has started to grow there that doesn't belong and is unproductive. Isn't it funny that you don't have to do anything to get weeds to grow in your garden? They will come up all by themselves, and they will choke out the good stuff, the stuff you actually want to see produced.

The same is true in our lives. We don't really have to do anything to see stuff appear that we know God doesn't want for us and that interferes with us having the life God has for us. We don't have to try to become self-focused. We don't have to try to live unholy. In our flesh, we will naturally gravitate toward sinful, ungodly behavior and thoughts. Just like weeds in a garden, behavior will spring up that can choke out the good stuff.

That's why we need the supernatural. We have to ask the Holy Spirit to clean up our lives by asking Him to call attention to the things that don't belong and are unproductive. It may be practices or habits that don't glorify God. It may be relationships that are choking out God's work in your heart. It may even be things that in themselves are not necessarily thought of as sinful, but they're still keeping you from God's best for your life. A. W. Tozer has rightly said:

> This is the aspect of the Christian life that most people do not like. They want comfort, blessing and peace, but they recoil from this radical, revolutionary break with the world. To follow Christ in this rough and thorough-going way is too much for them.[8]

Whatever it is and whatever the cost, it needs to be—it has to be—weeded out. If you will ask the Holy Spirit to bring it to the surface and clean it up, He will do just that as you yield to Him.

Built Up

Once the soil has been broken up and cleaned up, it needs to be built up. Soil can become depleted of the nutrients it needs for good production. Things like fertilizer and compost are added to the ground to build it up and enrich the soil so that maximum results can be produced.

You guessed it; you and I have to be enriched or built up by adding the Word of God into our lives on a daily basis. I'll have more to say about this later, but like the soil, our spirits can become depleted and unproductive. The Word of God provides the spiritual nutrients we so desperately need to see God produce His promises in us.

Opened Up

Next, the soil has to be opened up for the seeds. Plowing creates trenches in the ground that make the perfect environment for the seeds to be planted. Without plowing, the seed just falls on the top of the soil where it's exposed to the elements or where birds can come and snatch it up. For the greatest potential for a healthy crop, the farmer knows that the soil has to be opened up so that the seed can get down into it.

In our lives, in preparation to receive God's power, you and I have to be opened up. We have to be prepared to receive God's power into our lives. That usually means that God has to do some plowing in our lives to bring us to a place where His power can work.

Let me stop right here and say something that you probably already know but need to be reminded of: God's plowing in our lives can be a painful experience. That's why we have to always keep in mind that God loves us and has our best interests in mind. If we don't hang on to that truth and remind ourselves of it continually, then when the plowing starts, we may begin to question what God is doing. We can become angry or discouraged. Remember, when God begins plowing, it's because He wants to produce His fruit in our lives.

God's plowing may include conviction from the Holy Spirit concerning something in our lives that God wants to change. That's not fun. Very few of us like to have things pointed out in our lives that aren't right. In our flesh, our natural response is usually to deny it, defend it, or deflect it. (Have you ever read the story of King David and his sin with Bathsheba?) We come up with excuses. We act like we don't see it. We start looking at the faults and struggles of others. Everything in us fights against being opened up. We have to humble ourselves and accept God's conviction as the gift that it is.

At times, God may use the testimony of another person to open us up and make us more receptive to God's work because we hear how God worked in his or her life. It could be a sermon we hear or a devotional that we read. And it could also be a trial or circumstance that comes into our life that God can use to better prepare the spiritual soil of our life.

This last idea can be particularly hard for us to accept, partly because, well, because we just don't like going through trials. I don't know of anybody who does. But also, people have a hard time accepting the idea that God would actually use a trial or circumstance or adversity in their lives. The reason they sometimes have a hard time accepting that idea is because of a false theology that has been perpetuated in our culture from some of today's most prominent television preachers. It is the unbiblical notion that God wants only the very best for you.

Now before you slam this book closed in disgust because of my last statement, hear me out. God, our loving Father, does want the very best for each and every one of us. That is absolutely true. The problem is that some talk-show hosts and television preachers have taken it upon themselves to define what is God's best. They interpret it to mean that God wants the best only for your physical life here and now. And I'm sorry, but that's simply not true.

The idea that God always wants us to get the better-paying job, that He wants us to have the nicer house and drive the nicer car, that He never wants us to be sick, that idea of God's best is pushed like some sort of spiritual drug to make us feel good. And let's be honest; it sounds great, doesn't it? Who wouldn't want the nice job, the nice house, and the nice car? Who wouldn't want to be healthy and wealthy? Who wouldn't want easy circumstances all of the time?

The problem is, first, reality teaches us that it's simply not true. Even the people who do have the terrific job and beautiful big home and fancy car still have plenty of adversity and challenges in life. Trust me; after more than twenty years of ministering to people on all levels of the economic scale, the size of the house you live in or the number of figures in your salary cannot keep physical, emotional, and relational issues from coming into your life.

Second, and more importantly, the Bible tells us that's it's not true. From Genesis to Revelation, we find that it was the people who were the most committed to God and had the strongest faith who were the ones who usually faced the greatest adversity and challenges in their lives.

Think of all the biblical examples of faithful followers of God who experienced anything but the best life in this world. Abel was murdered by his brother because he offered a better sacrifice to God. Joseph was falsely accused of rape and languished in prison for years because he did not wish to dishonor God. Moses had to run for his life and live on the back side of the desert for forty years, working for his father-in-law. David had to hide in caves to escape jealous King Saul. Jeremiah was thrown into a dried-up well for preaching the truth. Mary, the mother of Jesus, faced public humiliation and rejection from her fiancé. All the apostles were killed or imprisoned for their faith. Paul spent several years in prison, received multiple beatings, was run out of town more times than he could probably remember, and was eventually beheaded! I wonder what these giants of the faith would say about today's peddlers of prosperity?

No, the truth is, God's best for His children will always put a priority on the eternal, not the temporal. Nice houses, nice cars, and a nice living are, well, nice. And there's nothing wrong with the temporal niceties of life. But all that stuff is destined for dust. It's passing away. It is the spiritual aspect of our lives that will last into eternity.

The adversity, challenges, and circumstances of life are also all passing away. The apostle Paul said this about the trials and hardships we face: "For momentary, light affliction is producing for us an eternal weight of glory far beyond all comparison" (2 Corinthians 4:17). So if the hardships that life can sometimes bring are only temporary, doesn't it make sense that the eternal God would use them to produce in us something that will last for eternity? It may not always be pleasant, but it's always profitable. If God has to plow our lives by allowing difficulty in our circumstances, He will do it. He loves us enough to do it. But always remember:

Your trial is temporary—you are not.

Filled up

So after the plowing is done and the soil is opened up, then, of course, the seed is placed into the prepared soil. This is an exciting time for the farmer because he's done everything he could to get the soil ready. It hasn't been easy to get to this point, but it's where he's wanted to get to ever since he started.

God's power is like the farmer's seed. When we've placed ourselves in position for God to do what He wants to do in our lives, as we talked about in the last chapter, then He prepares us for His power to work in us. And the results are guaranteed!

Covered Up

Now, in the farming analogy, after the seed is in the ground, it's covered up with soil to allow the seed to germinate and produce the intended results. Again, just like the earlier step of exposing or opening up the soil so that the seed can get down into the ground, it also must be covered so that the seed can germinate and produce.

For us, prayer is the covering we need to see God's promises produced. Prayer has to blanket our lives so that God's power and purposes can be achieved. Remember, we are praying, but it's God who is covering us through our prayer. Certainly there is much about prayer that is a mystery to us, but if we don't cover our lives with prayer, we'll miss out on the full potential for God's power to be realized in our daily lives.

Think about your own personal prayer life for a moment. What does that look like for you? Does most of your prayer life take place in the twenty minutes that you spend driving to work each morning? Or maybe it's just before you go to bed, and five minutes into it, you're fighting to keep your eyes open. The question isn't whether it's wrong to pray on your way to work or before bed. The question we need to ask is, is it enough? Would the farmer, who is absolutely dependent on the seed producing, be as flippant about covering the seed as we are about allowing God's prayer covering on our lives?

Spring Up

The final result, of course, is to begin to see the produce spring up out of the soil. This is the payoff for all the preparation that God has done in our lives. What an amazing and beautiful thing to see as the young tender plants begin to grow. And if we've allowed God's prep work to be accomplished in our lives, spiritually speaking, we can fully expect to see God's promises begin to spring up in our lives.

Okay, I promise I'm done with the planting analogy. That may have seemed like a lot, but we are talking about seeing results, after all. So preparation is the first part of the power pattern that you and I need for experiencing God's promises in our lives. Let's turn the page and take the next step toward living in the promises of God.

Chapter 8

How Do I Plan for It?

In the last chapter, we started looking at the need for a power pattern in our lives. That pattern begins with God's preparation of our lives. So now what? What do we do next after we've gotten into position for God's power and allowed Him to prepare us for His power?

Plan

How does the old saying go? "If you fail to plan, you plan to fail." It's astounding to me the number of professing followers of Jesus who give little to no thought about where they want to go in their spiritual walk or how they're going to get there. The truth is, most people put more planning into a trip to the grocery store than they put into their walk with Jesus. At least they make a list when they go to the grocery store!

Years ago I was watching television one night when this infomercial came on about how to buy and sell real estate. Cindi gets nervous when infomercials come on at our house because I've been accused of being a bit of a sucker for them.

I Get It!

I don't really think that's true, but hey, if we ever need to cut through an aluminum can and then slice tomatoes paper thin, we're set!

So I was watching this real estate infomercial hosted by this beautiful blonde (no doubt selected because of her vast real estate experience), and she was riding down a palm-tree-lined street in a convertible Rolls Royce, with mansions on both sides, designer sunglasses strategically reflecting the grandeur of the homes, hair gently blowing in the breeze but never enough to ruin the shot, and she was talking to this older, distinguished-looking gentleman, who was also wearing designer sunglasses as he drove through Beverly Hills and explained to me how my life was going to radically change for the better as a result of ordering his course. (I know, right? It's so realistic. How could you not believe it?)

To Cindi's relief, I didn't succumb to the temptation to become a real estate tycoon that night, but something that man said has stuck with me ever since I heard him say it and has helped me in my walk with Christ. I wasn't really expecting it, and I'm sure he didn't intend it, but this king of the infomercial real estate world had an impact on my spiritual life that night. As he drove under the swaying palm trees, down those sun-splashed streets with perfectly manicured lawns and pristine mansions, and attempted to convince me that this was the life I really wanted and could have if I would just order his "foolproof" course, he said something profound:

> *"Remember, if you aim at nothing, you will surely hit it."*

Okay, maybe you had to be there, but for me it was profound. How many followers of Jesus don't really aim at anything? They have this vague notion about wanting to please God and have a life like He says they can have, but they have no direction. They have no plan. As far as their spiritual lives are concerned, they're aiming at nothing. And they are surely hitting it!

Remember, the goal is to be in and stay in position to receive God's power so that His promises can be produced in your life. So make a plan! Now, I don't know that I would say that there's a "one size fits all" plan when it comes to your walk with Christ, but there certainly are some basic fundamentals that all of us should keep in mind.

Set Realistic Goals

Honestly, about the worst thing you could do is to become convicted about needing a plan and then set goals that set you up to fail. Don't get me wrong; there's certainly nothing wrong with godly conviction. God's trying to get our attention. He wants us to make changes. He wants us to go deeper with Him. But sometimes people set goals that they can't possibly keep in the long run.

It's what I call YCS, or "Youth Camp Syndrome." As a student pastor for a number of years, I saw this phenomenon appear time and again. Students would go off to summer camp with their student pastor. They were away from their TV, PC, and MCD, that's "Mobile Communication Device" (I just think it sounds way cooler than "cell phone"). The music was inspiring, the speaker made everybody (including himself) cry, and oftentimes the Holy Spirit moved in a powerful way.

That's great, and I'm not trying to make light of student camps or make fun of the speakers. I'd like to be one. But what often happens is that unrealistic goals are set, usually on the last night as everyone is crowded down at the front of the stage and emotions are running high. "I'm committing to reading my Bible every day for an hour and a half, followed by an hour and a half of prayer—and that's before I leave for school! I'm going to share my faith with six people a day, and I'm going to be a missionary in the Congo!"

Again, I applaud a person's desire to be all that God wants them to be, and we always need to respond to the Holy Spirit's prompting, but could you at least get through geometry before you start packing for the mission field? The problem is that when students, or anybody else for that matter, come back from their spiritual mountaintop experience (it could be a camp or a class or even an inspiring book), they have to go back down into the valley of their circumstances. And the goals they set during their spiritual mountaintop experience simply can't be maintained in the daily grind of life. Usually when we set those types of goals and then fail at them, we end up frustrated and less likely to even try again.

Why not set a goal that's a little more realistic? For instance, in your personal devotion time with God, what if you committed to read your Bible thirty minutes a day, followed by fifteen minutes of prayer, and you're going to do it five days a week so that you've got a couple of days to spare if you miss one during the week?

That may not sound very spiritual to you, and I'm certainly not advocating less time in prayer or the study of God's Word. But considering the fact that the average professing Christian probably spends less than three minutes a day total in prayer and/or Bible study, I'd say that's a vast improvement. As a pastor, I'd be ecstatic if I knew that the men and women of Cross Culture Church were all spending that much time in prayer and Bible study.

Plus remember, you can always go up. You can always raise the level of your commitments, and you should and will want to as you grow in Christ, but having to go backwards will always leave you feeling defeated. Be intentional, be committed, but be realistic.

Settle In

Americans don't like to wait. As a matter of fact, one of the biggest adjustments Americans have to make when they travel into other countries is understanding that other cultures aren't in nearly as big of a hurry as we are.

We have drive-through windows because we don't like to wait for our food. We have microwave popcorn because we don't like to wait for it to pop. We have twenty-minute workouts at the gym, high-speed Internet on our computers, and 4G networks on our smartphones, all designed to make our lives faster.

I'm sorry, but that's simply not how your spiritual life works. The Christian life is a marathon, not a sprint. Now it's true that none of us know how long we'll be here, and we shouldn't procrastinate; but remember, this is about a relationship with God, and you don't rush through a relationship. That's why I'm not really a big fan of those "read through the Bible in one year" plans. I know some people love them, and there is profit to them. I've even done them myself in the past. In my opinion, though, the danger is that there is potential to turn reading the Bible into an assignment, and a relationship isn't an assignment.

Have you ever gotten a love letter from someone, maybe a boyfriend or girlfriend? Do you remember how you felt when you saw that letter in the mailbox or someone handed it to you across the lunchroom table? Today it would more likely be an e-mail or a text, but do you remember the feeling of anticipation as you began to open the letter? Do you remember how you hung on each line and read it over and over and over again?

Well, guess what? The Bible is a love letter from God to us! In His love letter, God shows Himself to us. He reveals His character to us. God tells us of His love for us. God tells us about His plans for us and our future with Him. In His love letter, God tells us about the promises He has for us. I don't know of anybody who wants to rush through a love letter. Going to God's Word or praying isn't something we should do just so we can check off a box. We spend time in God's Word and we spend time talking to Him because we want to hang out with God, because we want to know God.

And maybe the most astounding thing about that truth is that God, the creator of all that is or ever will be, wants us to know Him! He invites us to come into His presence and learn from Him and learn about Him. Why would we ever rush that? Slow down. You don't have to have all the answers tomorrow; you won't anyway. One of the amazing things about having a relationship with the God of the universe is that you could spend a lifetime or ten thousand lifetimes getting to know Him and you'd never know everything there is to know about God!

Instead of thinking you have to read a different chapter every day, why not read the same chapter every day for a month? At the end of that month, if someone asks you how much of the Bible you've read, you may not be able to say you've read thirty chapters in the last thirty days (I've never had anybody ask me that anyway, have you?), but I'll bet you'll be able to tell someone about that one chapter, because you'll know it. And you'll know more about God. And knowing more about God helps you know God. And that's the objective.

What if you spend a whole year in one book of the Bible? Could that really be a bad thing? Are the Bible police going to come and arrest you for not reading more parts? Slow down. Settle in. Get to know God's Word and you'll get to know God. Get to know God and you'll begin to experience His promises in your life.

Set Time Aside

You have to decide when is the best time for you to spend with God and His Word, and you have to set that time aside to do it. Most of us lead busy lives with plenty to do. Most of us also know that the things that don't get scheduled usually end up getting canceled. It's what's sometimes referred to as "the tyranny of the urgent." We may have every good intention of spending time with God, but the busyness of life overwhelms those good intentions.

Might I also suggest that the best time to do this is early in the morning while most of your day is still in front of you, when you need God's power the most in your life, not at the end of your day when you're ready to go to sleep?

Of course, there can and probably will be more specifics to your plan as it develops, but setting realistic goals, settling in, and setting time aside are a great place to start. That may seem overly simplistic to you at this point, but despite what you may have thought in the past, God doesn't make this difficult. Life is difficult. Life is hard. But God invites you to come into His presence and begin to experience His promises in your life. You just have to get started, which brings us to the third part of the power pattern.

Practice

When I say you need to practice, I don't mean like a football team practices during the week to get ready for the real game on the weekend. I mean practice in the sense of a doctor who practices medicine. In other words, they do it. Doctors roll up their sleeves, put on their white coats and stethoscopes, park their Porsches in their assigned parking spaces, and go to work. (Sorry, I couldn't resist.)

At this point, it may sound a little like I'm contradicting myself, because earlier I told you not to rush, but I was referring to the idea of thinking you had to hurry through God's Word so that you could check off the box that says you did your quiet time. Like I said, that's not how you build a relationship. What I'm saying now is that it's time to get going! Move your feet! Start practicing!

> *You've got to set your mind to the task, set your excuses to the side, and set your alarm to go off!*

What this whole thing has been about is experiencing God's promises in your life. The sooner you get started by making sure you're in the right position and doing what's necessary to stay there, the sooner you'll begin to live in the reality of those promises. We'll come back to that in the next chapter, but remember:

> *The Christian life may be a marathon, but the runner who just stands at the starting line and keeps saying, "I really need to get going" is never going to get there.*

Now, there's one more part to this pattern for living in God's power and promises.

Persevere

I'd love to tell you that once you begin to implement this power pattern, it's all smooth sailing from then on out, but it's not. You'll have good days and bad days. Some days you'll do it all right and think you're beginning to get it, and other days you'll wonder why you even try. You can't quit. You have to get up and do it again tomorrow and the next day and the next.

Remember, your adversary, the devil, knows how dangerous you are when you begin to get it. He knows that not only will you begin to experience the promises of God, like peace, joy, contentment, and purpose in your life, but he also knows that people around you will begin to take notice of what's happening in your life. You will begin to become a walking billboard for Jesus, and that scares Satan very much. Here's why.

This was brought out in the first chapter of this book, but I believe that ultimately everybody is looking for the same things in life. Everybody wants to live without fear. Everybody wants true, lasting peace in his or her life. Everybody wants to believe his or her life has meaning and purpose. Of course, as we've already discussed, the world promises you can have it through riches or fame. You and I know that in the end, God is the only one who can deliver His promises. When we live in the reality of the power of God that produces the promises of God in our lives, we're like a giant neon arrow pointing at Jesus and saying, "This way to freedom! This way to hope! This way to peace and security! This way to real love! This way to true life!"

As you might imagine, Satan doesn't want to see that happen, so if he can, he'll get you to quit. He'll try to get you to throw in the towel, walk away, tap out, and go back to a type of Christianity that is unsatisfying, unfulfilling, unrewarding, and unproductive for you, unattractive to others, and undisturbing to him.

I've told a lot of people through the years that following Jesus in this life is always going to be like swimming against the current. That's just how it is. Jesus said, "In this world you will have tribulation" (John 16:33). In the book of James, we're told that we will encounter "various trials" (James 1:2).

If you've ever swum against the current in the ocean or up a stream, you know how exhausting it can be. After a while, your arms and legs feel like lead weights. Your lungs feel like they're going to explode, and all you want to do is quit. All that is necessary, however, to find yourself going in the wrong direction is to stop stroking, and the current will naturally take you back in the wrong direction.

The good news is that if you keep on swimming, it does get easier. The current is still working against you, but if you keep stroking, as you keep getting back into the water day after day and putting in your laps, something begins to happen to you. Your muscles begin to become stronger and more toned, your cardiovascular system becomes more proficient, your lung capacity expands, your body becomes leaner, and your technique becomes better. Like I said, you're still swimming against the current, but it's not nearly as hard as it once was. The only way the current wins is if you quit.

The same thing is true for the followers of Jesus who refuse to give in to their circumstances. As we continue to practice the disciplines needed in our lives that we've talked about, the power of God becomes more and more evident and effective in our lives. God's power begins to manifest itself in our lives, producing God's promises.

The only way your circumstances win is if you quit.

Don't quit. Persevere in your pursuit of an intimate relationship with God. Don't let Satan, your circumstances, or anything else keep you from what God wants for you to have in your relationship with Him. Persevere, and then watch what happens.

Chapter 9

Will I Know When I Get It?

A few years ago I got motorcycle fever. I had one when I was a kid, and I rode some motocross as a teenager, but I hadn't ridden in years. It's hard to say what sparked my renewed interest. My son Todd had gotten a street bike after he moved out, and whenever he came over we would talk about motorcycles some, so maybe that was part of it. Maybe part of it was watching too many episodes of Orange County Choppers. Maybe part of it was just what is referred to as the "middle-aged crazies." Whatever all the reasons might have been, I wanted one.

Thus began a three or four year odyssey of researching, gathering data, and looking at bikes. My family will tell you that I tend to not make decisions very quickly. That's not necessarily a bad thing. There's a lot to think about. *Do I want a sport bike? Do I want a touring bike? Do I want cruiser? Am I a Harley kind of guy?* (Some how I just couldn't see myself pulling off the bandana and wallet chain look.) At one point,

I Get It!

after looking at probably hundreds of bikes, Todd said to me, "Dad, it's time to pull the trigger or put the gun down."

I eventually did "pull the trigger." I got the bike that was perfect for me. I got the boots. I got the jacket. I got the gloves. I got the helmet. (You've got to love craigslist!) I possessed everything I needed to be a motorcyclist. But I wasn't a motorcyclist, not really, not until I actually began to ride.

As I've said throughout this book if you have a personal relationship with Jesus Christ then you already have inside of you the power you need to live in the promises of God, because God the Holy Spirit dwells in you. You probably also have access to His word. And, even though you didn't necessarily have to, you've even purchased this book and invested the time to read it. But, like motorcycling and me, possessing everything needed to live in the promises of God doesn't mean that you do. You won't really get it until you start to live it.

To be perfectly honest, if you don't get it, it's not my fault. I cringe even as I write those words because I know that must sound incredibly arrogant. It sounds that way to me and I wrote it! I don't mean it to sound that way. I'm under no delusions of grandeur that I'm God's gift of literary genius to the world. What I'm trying to say is that God is the one who has promised things like forgiveness, eternal life, peace, purpose, power, hope, joy, meaning, love, and all the rest. I didn't promise those things to you—God did!

God is not some kind of cosmic prankster who promises you all these things that will make your life truly what it was meant to be and then pulls the proverbial chair out from under you. "Psych! I was only kidding. I don't want you to have a life of joy. I don't want you to experience My peace. I want you to be filled with stress, anxiety, fear, doubt, hopelessness, uncertainty, guilt, and whatever else I can think of to make your life miserable!"

No, as I've already said, and more importantly as His Word makes clear, God wants you to have His promises. You're His child, and God loves you. God wants you to live in the reality of His promises. God wants you to have life more abundant. God wants you to have what He created you to have! What I've tried to do through this book is to remind you of what God's Word says about living in the reality of God's promises, reveal to you why you don't have it, and then restore your hope and confidence that you really can have what God wants you to have. After that, it really comes down to what you're going to do.

God's word is clear. Anyone can get it as long as they take the steps necessary and don't quit. Quite frankly, whether you get it or not depends on whether you're willing to believe God enough to take those steps to experience this life He has promised. In other words, to "get it," you're going to have to "do it."

So what does "it" look like when you get it? Let me introduce you to Jean. Back when I worked for the post office, I would sometimes deliver mail to Jean. When I knew her, Jean was perhaps in her fifties or sixties, but as a young girl, she had contracted a disease that over time left her legs and hands disfigured and without function, and often with a great deal of pain. Jean lived alone in a little wooden house on a dead-end street behind a grocery store. She spent her days in a hospital-type bed inside a bedroom, maybe six by eight feet at best, with a small window above her bed.

Someone would come in for part of the day and prepare meals for Jean and do the things that had to be done for her, but basically, Jean's days were spent in that little bed, inside that little room, inside that little house, on that little dead-end street behind the grocery store.

None of us—and I mean none of us—would want Jean's circumstances. Nobody in his or her right mind would ask to go through what Jean had to go through every single day of her life—but every one of us would be better off if we had Jean's outlook on life. I have rarely, if ever, met someone as joyous, as content, and as full of life as Jean. She loved to smile. She loved to laugh. And Jean loved to talk about Jesus.

She always had words of encouragement for those who came to visit her, and she never talked about her trials or circumstances. If you went to visit Jean, you might think you were blessing her, and no doubt she appreciated the visit; but you always left Jean's house knowing that you were the one who had really been blessed.

Almost every day after school, neighborhood children would go over to Jean's house. She had someone put cookies out before the children got there. All the kids would cram into that little bedroom, and Jean would read them Bible stories and ask them about their day. She would laugh and smile and tell each of them how special they were and how much God loved them.

I have no doubt that Jean lived with a fair amount of pain on a daily basis, but you would never know it being around her. There was a joy, a peace, and a contentment to Jean's life that defies logic. How could anybody enjoy a life trapped in such circumstances? How could anybody smile and laugh in the face of such adversity? Was Jean delusional? Was she living in denial? Or could it be something else? Is it possible that Jean was actually living in the reality of God's promises, promises that aren't tied to life's situations or our circumstances, but are able to meet us right smack-dab in the middle of them and give us victory over whatever life throws at us?

Jean's body may have been trapped in that room, but her life certainly wasn't. Jean got it. Her life had meaning and purpose. Her life was productive. She lived in the presence and with the peace and power of the Holy Spirit on a daily basis. She had a ministry that touched hundreds if not thousands of lives through the years. She laughed, she loved, and she lived.

Jean lived in the reality of the apostle Paul's words: "I know what it is to be in need, and I know what it is to have plenty. I have learned the secret of being content in any and every situation, whether well fed or hungry, whether living in plenty or in want. I can do all this through him who gives me strength" (Philippians 4:12–13 NIV).

I've known of men and women who make millions of dollars, live in magnificent houses, drive fancy cars, and travel the world, but they have never experienced the peace and contentment that Paul describes in those verses and that Jean experienced in her life every single day.

Ironically enough, the Beatles made a lot of money off the song "Can't Buy Me Love" (referring to money), but the truth is, money can't buy you any of the things that you really want out of life. Oh, to be sure, money can buy you toys. Money can buy you entertainment. Money can buy you experiences, but money can't buy you real peace or fulfillment or even contentment. For most people, the things that money can buy simply act as band aids, covering up the wounds of a discontented and dissatisfied life, but never giving them lasting peace, joy, and satisfaction in life.

Jean's life, like Paul's (the apostle, not the Beatle), was the proof that when you place yourself in position for the power of God to operate in your life, the promises of God leap off the pages of the Bible and actually become a reality for you. Jean may not have been able to control her circumstances, but she absolutely did not allow her circumstances to control her. And you and I don't have to let our circumstances control us either. Circumstances may bring challenges to our lives, but they don't have to control them.

You can't fake it

So how do you know if you've got it? Well, let me first say that you can't fake it, not for very long anyway. Acting happy or putting on a big smile and saying, "Praise the Lord!" simply won't be enough to get you through the trials of life. It might fool the church crowd you hang out with once or twice a week, but your family, your neighbors, and your coworkers probably know the truth. And deep down inside, so do you.

I like watches. Anybody who knows me knows that's true. Yes, one is all you really need, and I know collecting watches could make some guys question whether I ought to turn in my man card, but I like them. I think there's a running bet at church as to which watch I'm going to be wearing each Sunday.

Now, for the record, I don't really have that many watches, and before you judge me, ladies, should we count how many pairs of shoes are in your closet? If you happen to be a "watchaholic" like I am, you know that some watches cost tens of thousands of dollars. Of course, none of my watches are anywhere near that expensive.

The one exception is my Breitling. That's right; I have a Breitling, which watch aficionados will instantly recognize as a high-end watch. In the world of watches, Breitling is to Timex what Aston Martin is to Kia. My apologies to both Timex and Kia, who make fine products, but it's just a different class.

I was wearing my Breitling one day when my neighbor, who owns a Rolex, came by. I could instantly tell by the flash in his eyes and the flare in his nostrils that this was perceived as a threat to his neighborhood "chrono supremacy." He was admiring my watch the way one gunfighter admires another gunfighter's gun and wondering the whole time, *Who's really the best?* It was like that scene from *Rocky IV* where Rocky and the Russian, Drago, stand toe-to-toe, face-to-face in the ring before the big fight: "I must break you." "Go for it."

I just knew that at any second, he was going to challenge me to compare second-hand movements or bracelet-clasping types. (Come to think of it, maybe I do need to turn in my man card!)

But alas, my running with the herd of upper-echelon watch wearers ended the same way it always does, by my admitting to my neighbor, "It's a fake." That's right; I'm a watch poser. I could see the relief instantly pass over my neighbor's face. He was still top watch in the neighborhood.

I get a lot of compliments, though, when I wear my Breitling knockoff. It's a good-looking watch. But inevitably, I tell them the truth, which is that it came, not from some high-end jewelry store on Rodeo Drive for thousands of dollars, but from a back-alley street merchant in Hong Kong for twenty-five bucks.

The reason I always end up telling people is because I fear that sooner or later, if they look close enough, they're going to find out the truth anyway. Sure, from a distance, my watch looks great, but if you look close enough, you can tell it's a fake.

I believe that describes a lot of our lives. We smile and sing the songs. We give the expected response: "I'm doing great! How are you doing?" We act like we've got it all together; our family is perfect, our marriage is perfect, our life is perfect. From a distance, everything looks great, but we know that if people get close enough, they'll discover the truth. It's a fake. It's a façade.

I'm convinced that desire to fake it is at least part of the reason for the enormous popularity and success of Facebook, Twitter, MySpace, Instagram, and other social networking sites. It's relationships at a distance. It's relationships that I have much more control over and can show people only the aspects of my life that I want them to see. I don't have to let them get too close. I can fake it.

Hopefully, by now you understand that it doesn't have to be that way. We can live authentic lives that are full and purposeful and content. We can live with peace and joy and without fear and anxiety—not because I say so in this book, but because God says so in His book. Life really can be abundant. We don't have to fake it.

You can't make it

So still we're left with the question, where's the proof? How do we know when we've got it? Well, in some sense, it's so obvious that it doesn't even really need to be stated. Like the road sign I saw that read, "Caution, water on road during rain," some things are just so obvious that they go without saying. So if you have to ask if you've got it, then you probably don't.

Nevertheless, I believe the Bible tells us exactly what it looks like, and the answer is found in the apostle Paul's letter to the Galatians: "But the Holy Spirit produces this kind of fruit in our lives: love, joy, peace, patience, kindness, goodness, faithfulness, gentleness, and self-control. There is no law against these things! Those who belong to Christ Jesus have nailed the passions and desires of their sinful nature to his cross and crucified them there" (Galatians 5:22–24 NLT).

Did you notice that it's the Holy Spirit (we talked about Him back in chapter 4) who produces this fruit? It is His fruit. This isn't you or I trying to work up or create love, joy, peace, or any of the other attributes mentioned. As I've already said, we just don't have what it takes to produce long-term results. You and I can't make peace, joy, and contentment. This is God the Holy Spirit working in our lives to produce those attributes that give us the life God intended.

You just have to take it

I don't mean that heading to sound arrogant or presumptuous, but if you take the steps that we've looked at in this book and tap into the Holy Spirit's power, you will see His fruit produced in your life. That's one of God's promises! It is His power that produces His promises. He wants you to get it. You just have to put yourself in position to take it.

By the way, did you notice that the noun *fruit* in Galatians 5 is singular? It's not the "fruits" of the Spirit. In other words, it's a package deal. All the characteristics mentioned are what the Holy Spirit produces in our lives when we are surrendered to Him. Look at that list again. Imagine your life on a daily basis filled with love, joy, peace, patience, kindness, goodness, faithfulness, gentleness, and self-control. Imagine what that must feel like. Imagine the security when you live in the reality of His love. Imagine having abiding peace. Imagine having God-empowered patience for the daily stuff of life. Imagine all those characteristics becoming characteristics that people would use to describe your life—not for a few fleeting seconds now and then, but daily, continually, permanently!

Now try to imagine any circumstance, any trial, any hardship, or any difficulty that you might encounter in your life that you could not handle if the fruit of the Holy Spirit listed in Galatians 5 was characteristic of your life. Isn't that what the apostle Paul had? Isn't that what Jean had? Isn't that what you really want? Then it's time to stop imagining and start experiencing!

Christian artist Michael Card's song "Joy in the Journey" captures the essence of what it means to get it. The song says in part:

> There is a joy in the journey,
>
> There's a light we can love on the way.
>
> There is a wonder and wildness to life,
>
> And freedom for those who obey.[9]

That last line is particularly poignant and gets to the heart of what it takes to get it. The Christian faith is filled with what from a human, temporal perspective appears to be contradictions. To live, you have to die. If you want to find your life, you have to lose it. To receive, you have to give. And, as Michael Card so poetically reminds us, to be free, you have to obey.

None of those truths make sense to a world and culture absorbed with self and deceived by Satan. Doing it God's way will always run counter to that culture, but as I've said many times through the years to people struggling to choose between the pull of this world and the promises of God, you just have to decide who you're going to believe: a culture that is constantly trying to convince you that the trappings of this world hold the key to happiness, or the God who created you and loves you so much that He would rather die than live without you.

In the introduction of this book, I talked about an encounter I had a number of years ago with well-known pastor and author Dr. Charles Stanley and how that encounter became the inspiration for this book. Looking back on it years later, I'm convinced this is what Dr. Stanley was trying to help me understand that night over dinner. I think he wanted me to understand, both for myself and for those I would someday pastor and teach, that followers of Jesus don't have to live life like everybody else. We really can have joy in our journey. We really can have the promises of God and experience the life more abundant that Jesus promised. We really can "get it."

The ancient Chinese philosopher Lao-tzu is attributed with the statement, "A journey of a thousand miles begins with the first step." As I understand it, a literal rendering of the Chinese would be, "A journey of a thousand miles begins under your feet."[10] In other words, you're right where you need to be to get to where you want to go. But you have to get started. If you want to get it, then you're going to have to get on with it.

Why not begin to take the steps we've talked about? Those steps include making sure you are plugged into the power source by having a relationship with God, not just a religion about God. It also includes making sure you are in the right position to receive His promises by choosing a life of holiness instead of happiness, and surrender instead of service. We also talked about the preparation and planning needed for living in the promises of God.

So what are you waiting for? What's keeping you from grabbing hold of the life God intended for you? The promises that God has for you that lead to the life God wants for you are just too important to put off any longer. Why not go get it? As John Tillotson has said:

> To be always intending to live a new life, but never to find time to set about it; this is as if a man should put off eating, and drinking, and sleeping, from one day and night to another, till he is starved and destroyed.[11]

Someone has said:

> *"Procrastination is suicide on the installment plan."*

Manager and author Alyce P. Cornyn-Selby has said:

> *"Procrastination is, hands down, our favorite form of self-sabotage."*[12]

That's certainly true when it comes to living in the reality of the promises of God, because if you have a personal relationship with Jesus Christ, there is nothing in the universe that can keep God from delivering on His promises to you. His power, His peace, His joy, and all the other promises that make up the abundant life are yours for the taking.

To be honest, the only thing keeping you from getting it is you. Remember, every day that you wait is one more day that you don't get to live the life God wants you to have. And you have only so many days to this life. So to borrow a line from that great American philosopher Larry the cable guy, "Get 'er done!"

Endnotes

1. Wilbur Rees, "$3.00 Worth of God," *When I Relax I Feel Guilty*, Tim Hansel (Elgin, IL, David C. Cook Publishing Co., 1979), p. 49.

2. Steven Curtis Chapman and Phil Naish, *More to This Life* (Brentwood, TN: Sparrow Records, 1989).

3. Noel Langley, Florence Ryerson, Edgar Allan Woolf, *The Wonderful Wizard of Oz*, directed by Victor Fleming (1939, Los Angeles, Metro-Goldwyn-Mayer).

4. Billy Joel, "Only the Good Die Young," *The Stranger* (New York: Columbia, 1977).

5. Steven Curtis Chapman, "For the Sake of the Call" (Brentwood, TN: Sparrow Records, 1990).

6. Philip Kaufman, Sonia Chernus, *The Outlaw Josey Wales*, directed by Clint Eastwood, (1976, Los Angeles, Warner Bros.).

7. Ron Lee Davis, *Becoming a Whole Person in a Broken World* (Grand Rapids, MI: Discovery House, 1990), p. 152.

8. A. W. Tozer, *The Set of the Sail* (Camp Hill, PA: Christian Publications, 1986), p. 171.

9. Michael Card, "Joy in the Journey" (Brentwood TN: Sparrow Records, 1994).

10. Lao-tzu, *The Way of Lao-tzu*, (www.quotationspage.com, 2/4/14).

11. John Tillotson, (www.winwisdom.com, 4/9/14).

12. Alyce P. Cornyn-Selby, (www.thinkexist.com, 4/15/14).

CPSIA information can be obtained at www.ICGtesting.com
Printed in the USA
BVOW02s1146101014

370228BV00002B/7/P